THE ARTHRITIS COOKBOOK

THE ARTHRITIS COOKBOOK

OVER 50 DELICIOUS AND HEALTHY
RECIPES FOR PEOPLE WITH ARTHRITIS

MICHELLE BERRIEDALE-JOHNSON

LORENZ BOOKS

This edition published in 2000 by Lorenz Books

Lorenz Books is an imprint of
Anness Publishing Inc.
27 West 20ᵗʰ Street
New York, NY 10011
(800) 354-9657

A CIP catalogue record for this book is available from the British Library.

Publisher: Joanna Lorenz
Executive Editor: Linda Fraser
Project Editor: Rebecca Clunes
Designer: Ian Sandom
Recipes by: Carla Capalbo, Lesley Chamberlain, Jacqueline Clark, Carole Clements,
Andi Clevely, Roz Denny, Joanna Farrow, Nicola Graimes, Christine Ingram,
Peter Jordan, Lesley Mackley, Sally Mansfield, Sallie Morris, Katherine Richmond,
Liz Trigg, Lara Washburn, Stephen Wheeler, Elizabeth Wolf-Cohen, Jeni Wright
Photographer for introduction section: Janine Hosegood; Gettyone Stone (pp 6, 7, 15,
18, 19 top); Smith & Nephew Homecraft Ltd (21 top and left)
Photographers for recipes: James Duncan, John Freeman, Ian Garlick, Michelle Garrett,
Amanda Heywood, Dave Jordan, Dave King, William Lingwood, Michael Michaels,
Thomas Odulate, Sam Stowell
Typesetter: Diane Pullen
Nutritional Analysis: Clare Brain
Indexer: Hilary Bird

1 3 5 7 9 10 8 6 4 2

CONTENTS

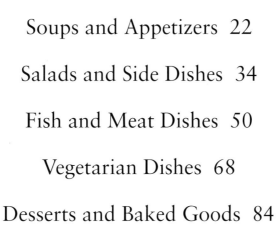

INTRODUCTION

Arthritis is a condition that can affect any of the joints, but it is especially prevalent in the load-bearing or particularly hardworking areas, such as the knees, hips, ankles, wrists and hands. In the Western world, it is estimated that up to half the population will suffer from an arthritic disorder of the joints at some point, and that many of these people will be severely troubled by constant pain, stiffness and disability. This is obviously a depressing prospect.

Arthritis cannot be treated as a single disease. There are at least six common forms and up to 100 lesser known types, excluding the rheumatic ailments that are often confused with arthritis. Although it is just as painful as arthritis, rheumatism (including fibrositis/fibromyalgia, bursitis, frozen shoulder and aching neck) is a less serious condition affecting muscles, ligaments and tendons.

Human joints are extremely complex and flexible structures, but they require "good maintenance" for efficient, long-term function. It is when a joint is damaged that arthritis can set in. Damage can be caused by a wide variety of incidents: trauma or accident, abnormal stress, maybe even viral infection or an inflammation. Confusingly, damage may not always lead to arthritis and, as yet, beyond a genetic predisposition, doctors have been unable to identify why some people develop arthritis-related conditions while others do not.

THE STRUCTURE OF A JOINT

A joint is made up of two connecting bones, separated and cushioned by cartilage. Cartilage is water-filled, spongy tissue with no blood vessels and no nerve endings, so cartilage itself never hurts. The joint is held together by a tubular structure attached to the ends of the bones. This is lined with a synovial membrane and lubricated by synovial fluid, which allows the moving parts to rub against each other with minimum friction. The joint is stabilized by muscles, ligaments and tendons on both its inside and outside.

CHANGES IN A DAMAGED AND ARTHRITIC JOINT

The protective cartilage is vital to the proper functioning of the joint. If the cartilage is damaged in any way it is less efficient as the cushion separating the bones.

When the cartilage ceases to perform its cushioning function properly there are several consequences. Initially there appears to be some water loss, after which the cartilage thickens and then softens. Small rips may appear and gradually deepen into tears, which may extend as far as the bone. The bone ends may be damaged, or the joint capsule and synovial membrane may become damaged or inflamed. The surrounding tendons and ligaments may also be strained. Eventually, the bone attempts to repair the damage by forming bone spurs, and these stretch the sensitive membrane covering the bone to visibly deform the joints, causing further strain on the surrounding membranes and muscles. The synovial lining, fluid and capsule become inflamed and the joint stiffens.

Although the cartilage has no feeling, the other parts of the joint, including the bone, are very sensitive. Increasing pain and stiffness lead to immobility, and experience shows that immobility only makes the condition worse. This explains why most arthritis sufferers find their condition more painful in the morning after lying still all night, than later in the day after moving around.

Left: Osteoarthritis often occurs in the joints that bear the most stress. Gardeners may find arthritis particularly painful in their knees, due to long hours of weeding.

Right: Arthritis can affect people of any age, even children. Juvenile arthritis can be particularly distressing, but the good news is that most children outgrow the condition, with no long-term effects.

TYPES OF ARTHRITIS

Although arthritis can take many different forms, the basic joint problem is the same for each type.

OSTEOARTHRITIS

This is the most common form of arthritis, usually associated with increasing age and degeneration. It is also more common in women. Osteoarthritis often occurs in a joint that has been injured or stressed, particularly those joints that do the most work—fingers and thumbs, wrists, knees, hips, ankles and toes. Bony spurs form around the joints and, along with inflammation, make movement difficult and painful.

Progressive joint deterioration can create secondary problems, such as carpal tunnel syndrome, which occurs when arthritis of the wrist causes nerves to be pinched. This produces pain, weakness and loss of control in the hands. Arthritis of the neck can cause severe headaches. Arthritis of the spine can cause radiating pain into the arm or leg (known as sciatica), or injury to the spinal column or the nerves within the spinal canal.

RHEUMATOID ARTHRITIS

This condition tends to occur in younger people. It is very dramatic and unpredictable and has been known to disappear as suddenly as it appears. It causes inflammation, pain, swelling and joint damage, especially in the hands and wrists, feet, knees and elbows. In severe cases rheumatoid arthritis can affect the internal organs—lungs, heart, liver, kidneys and lymph nodes.

Although no single cause has been found for rheumatoid arthritis, there is evidence to suggest that food allergies, nutritional deficiencies and viral,

parasitic and bacterial infections contribute to the condition.

ANKYLOSING SPONDILITIS

This is an inflammatory condition of the lower back, and it can spread both up and down the spine. It is most common in men.

JUVENILE ARTHRITIS

Symptoms include pain, fever, swelling and skin rash. The condition seems to improve over time, leaving the child with little serious joint damage.

PSORIATIC ARTHRITIS

A condition in which psoriasis (patches of raised, flaky and itching skin) and arthritis are combined.

VIRAL ARTHRITIS

This illness can follow a viral infection, whether or not the person already suffers from arthritis.

LUPUS ERYTHEMATOSUS

This condition causes inflammation of the connective tissue. Symptoms are influenza-like, including aching muscles and joints, fever and fatigue.

GOUT

This is caused by an excess of uric acid in the system. The acid crystals are deposited around joints and tendons, causing inflammation and pain. It can usually be controlled by drugs and by avoiding purines (substances rich in uric acid), which are found in liver, kidneys, shellfish, sardines, anchovies and beer.

TREATING ARTHRITIS

Conventional medicine, on the whole, does not accept a link between food and arthritis. However, there is some evidence to suggest that food intolerance and micro-nutrition (essential vitamins, minerals and trace elements) may play a significant role, especially in cases of rheumatoid arthritis.

CONVENTIONAL TREATMENT

Despite the fact that many people are disabled by the various forms of arthritis, medical science can offer no cure. Treatment therefore falls into four areas.

• **Minimizing stress on affected joints** Patients are often advised to lose weight. Although no one is quite sure why, it would appear that being overweight can negatively affect joints, including those that are not weight-bearing (fingers and wrists).

• **Keeping affected joints mobile** Regular, gentle exercise and physiotherapy will keep joints as supple as possible.

• **Reducing the pain of arthritis** Various pain-relieving drugs are used, normally corticosteroids and non-steroidal anti-inflammatory drugs (NSAIDs). Although they may relieve at least some of the inflammation and pain, they do nothing to reverse, or even slow down, the progress of the disease. These drugs can have serious side effects. Even short-term use of steroids can cause weight gain, the one thing that arthritics do not want. Long-term use can cause brittle bone disease or osteoporosis, muscle wasting, skin eruptions and damage, poor wound healing, fluid retention, eye disorders, nutritional deficiencies and even mental disturbance. NSAIDs most frequently cause stomach ulceration.

• **Clearing up infections** Some forms of arthritis (for example, certain cases of rheumatoid arthritis) seem to be set off by bacteria, such as salmonella, campylobacter or yersinai. Joint pains can linger for months or years. In such cases antibiotic treatment may be useful.

ALTERNATIVE TREATMENT

There are occasional cases where dramatic results are achieved by the exclusion or inclusion of one particular food in the diet. However, most people will find that a combined approach, following some of the suggestions below, will result in an improvement in their symptoms, if not a total cure.

• **Dietary manipulation of inflammation** This means eating foods that are most likely to reduce inflammation in the joints.

• **Vitamin and mineral supplementation** Eating a diet rich in the vitamins and minerals needed to minimize the damage caused by arthritis, while taking supplements to counteract possible deficiencies.

• **Exclusion diet** Pinpointing and then removing a particular food, such as wheat or tomatoes, that triggers arthritis or makes the symptoms worse.

• **Weight control** Following a diet to keep body weight down.

OTHER CAUSES

As with most other illnesses, stress seems to make arthritis worse and prevents healing, so minimizing stress is an important part of both complementary and conventional forms of treatment.

There is also some evidence to suggest that, although imbalance in the intestinal flora (an overgrowth of the yeast *candida albicans*) will not actually cause arthritis, it may well make the symptoms worse.

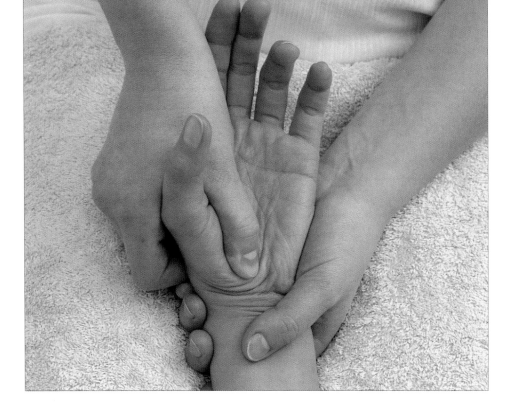

Left: A doctor will often recommend physiotherapy for joints affected by arthritis, as immobility only aggravates the condition. A gentle massage will help to keep your joints as supple as possible.

LOSING WEIGHT

This is a universal recommendation in the treatment of all types of arthritis, and so you need to make it a priority when you are planning your diet. Many of the dietary recommendations for weight loss will also help to reduce inflammation or increase antioxidant levels.

Most dieticians recommend a gradual weight loss, increasing your intake of vegetables, pulses and some grains, while reducing the fat content of your diet, especially animal fats. In addition, reducing the amount of sugar and refined white flour in a diet will often cause people to begin to lose weight.

Reducing the intake of sugar and refined flours does not need to eliminate the prospect of desserts. Fruits such as dates, prunes, raisins, apples and pears are excellent for sweetening desserts, and there are many flours, from whole-wheat flour to rice and chickpea flour, which are just as versatile as ordinary white flour.

NEW COOKING METHODS

Adjusting the way food is cooked is one easy way to reduce the use of cooking oils.

Deep-fried foods should be banned from the menu. Occasional shallow-frying in a little olive oil with a tablespoon of water added (to prevent the oil from overheating) is fine, but it is amazing how often broiling, roasting, poaching, steaming, baking or simmering can be used instead of frying. If you are still eating meat, broil sausages, bacon, fish and burgers. Eggs taste delicious poached. Potatoes can be baked or steamed, or, if you are really desperate for French fries, treat yourself to an occasional plate of baked fries, which are much lower in fat. Casseroles—for which ingredients are usually first fried in oil—often taste just as good if this step is omitted. Simply combine all the ingredients and cook the whole dish a little longer at a lower temperature, so as to let the flavors mature.

Vegetables are much better steamed than boiled, as this cooking method

does not allow so many nutrients to leach out and the vegetables have less opportunity to overcook.

Sweating is another good cooking method. This needs only a very small amount of oil (about 1 tablespoon) with 1 tablespoon water. Put the vegetables, oil and water into a saucepan with a tight-fitting lid and cook them slowly in their own juices. You will lose very few of the nutrients, apart from some Vitamin C, which will be lost no matter what your cooking method.

EATING LESS MEAT

Vegetarians seem to have less trouble with arthritis than people who eat meat, so there is an argument for trying to reduce the overall consumption of meat. If the idea of a totally vegetarian diet does not appeal, there are a number of meat substitutes that taste fine. TVP (textured vegetable protein) has a texture similar to chicken and, like plain tofu, is relatively tasteless but

Above: Fatty foods, especially meat and cooking fats derived from animals, can increase the swelling and pain in arthritic joints.

absorbs other flavors well. It can be used with marinades, in curries, casseroles or stews with plenty of herbs and strongly-flavored vegetables. Tofu is also available smoked and marinated and can be used in stir-fries, risottos, pilafs, bean dishes and salads with a good strong dressing (this is a good opportunity to use some inflammation-reducing oil).

Include some totally vegetarian meals in your weekly diet. A good selection of vegetables, roasted with some herbs and nuts, is an excellent and very easy dish. Dishes made with beans, nuts, seeds, herbs, spices and seaweed (which are now fairly easy to obtain and have a wonderful flavor) are exciting, filling, healthy— and not fattening!

REDUCING INFLAMMATION

Inflammation is the body's way of bringing extra blood, with all its healing nutrients, to an injured area of the body. In the case of arthritis the extra blood, far from healing the injury, creates extra heat and swelling, which merely add to the stiffness and soreness of the joint.

The inflammation of the joints that is associated with arthritis can be triggered, often on an ongoing basis, by damage to some part of the joint. Another possible cause is a malfunction in the body's mechanisms for triggering inflammation.

Various foods, especially fats, can influence the inflammatory process in either a negative or a positive way. This is because the chemicals (prostaglandins) that control inflammation are derived from fats in the body. Prostaglandin E2 is the chemical that sparks the inflammation; it is derived mainly from the fats found in meat and cooking oils. Prostaglandins E1 and E3 act in quite the opposite way, to block swelling and reduce the pain and heat. Prostaglandin E1 is derived from gamma linolenic acid (GLA) found only in a few seed oils—borage, evening primrose, black currant and hemp/linseed. Prostaglandin E3 is derived from alpha linolenic acid (ALA) and is found in green leafy vegetables, canola oil, wheatgerm oil and oily fish.

Although these fats do not work in exactly the same way for everyone, decreasing the amount of fat in the diet from animal sources and cooking oils and increasing plant foods, seeds and oily fish may help to reduce inflammation without the unwanted side effects caused by drugs. This is one of the reasons why many arthritics find a vegetarian or vegan diet, free of animal products, helpful.

GAMMA LINOLENIC ACID (GLA)

Eating more seeds and seed oils is the easiest way to increase GLA intake to make the inflammation-reducing prostaglandins. Evening primrose, borage and black currant oils can all be taken in capsule form, but hemp, or linseed, oil has to be consumed as an oil, and this, unfortunately, has an unpleasant taste. There is one seed oil blended by a Canadian, Professor Udo

Above: Cod liver oil or cod liver oil capsules are an excellent way of boosting your intake of ALAs, which in turn may help to control the inflammation caused by arthritis.

Erasmus, an acknowledged expert on the role of fats in the diet and in degenerative diseases such as arthritis. Known as Udo's Oil, it tastes pleasant enough to be used as a salad oil and, although expensive, it is an excellent way of boosting GLA intake.

Eating pumpkin, sunflower and sesame seeds, and linseeds, will also help to boost your intake—they can be eaten as they are or added to almost any dish. Use the seeds whole, when they will have to be chewed well to release the oils, or process them briefly in a mortar and pestle, coffee grinder or a food processor. Whole seeds can be lightly toasted under the broiler to vary their flavor.

Left: Some seeds contain useful amounts of helpful GLAs. Try to use a handful of seeds in every meal. Clockwise from top: sunflower seeds, linseeds, sesame seeds and pumpkin seeds.

ALPHA LINOLENIC ACID (ALA)

Reducing your intake of animal fats usually means eating more fresh fruits and vegetables—which boosts consumption of alpha linolenic acid (ALA), used to manufacture prostaglandin E3. Wheatgerm oil supplement will further boost alpha linolenic acid intake—but this is not suitable for those excluding wheat from their diet. Eating oily fish is also a good way to increase ALA in the diet. The term "oily" fish may sound rather unattractive, but, in fact, sardines, anchovies, mackerel, salmon, herrings, kippers and whitebait are some of the tastiest of seafoods. Most can be bought in a form where you do not have to deal with fish bones or skin, and some types can be eaten whole. Pre-prepared fish can be bought fresh, frozen or canned. As well as using oily fish as main courses, add them in small amounts to salads and rice, bean or

vegetable dishes. Try using anchovies to season some of your dishes instead of salt. As well as boosting your ALA levels, you will be reducing your sodium intake and helping to control high blood pressure.

GINGER

This spice has been used for centuries in traditional Indian Ayurvedic medicine as an anti-inflammatory food. It blocks the enzymes that make the inflammation-producing prostaglandins. Ginger does not work for everyone, but a dose of 1–2 grams of ground ginger or a 2-ounce piece of fresh ginger, peeled and grated, taken daily over a period of 3–4 months, appears to produce very positive results in the symptoms of over half the people who try it.

If you like ginger, you can consume it as a drink (there are a number of herbal teas with ginger), in ginger wine or as a confection, coated in chocolate. Ground ginger can be used in cakes and cookies, and fresh ginger root is delicious in a wide variety of savory dishes. You can even eat crystallized or stem ginger in ice cream.

Below: Oily fish are some of the best foods for reducing inflammation. It is, however, sometimes hard to know which fish belong to this category. Tuna, for instance, is not an oily fish. Clockwise from bottom left: tuna steak, mackerel, herring, salmon steak.

INCREASING VITAMINS AND MINERALS

Even with a balanced and healthy diet, "micro-nutrient malnutrition" may occur, especially as people grow older. This can either be the result of a deficiency of vitamins and minerals in the diet, or of the body's failure to absorb these substances properly from food.

If bones and joints are not receiving enough of the vitamins and minerals needed to maintain them, they are more likely to degenerate. Taking a "broad spectrum" supplement or a multi-vitamin and mineral supplement is helpful, but it may be worth consulting a nutritionist and having a blood test to assess whether the body is deficient in any specific mineral. Iron, zinc, copper, selenium and manganese are all important minerals for joint health, and their absorption can be impeded by consuming too much tea, coffee and bran. The traditional arthritis remedy of wearing a copper bracelet can be helpful, as small amounts of copper can be absorbed through the skin.

FREE RADICALS

Most people have heard of free radicals in connection with cancer; they are also relevant in arthritis. As oxygen is processed through the bloodstream and into the tissues, free radical chemicals (including hydrogen peroxide) are released. Although these free radicals are very unstable and only exist for 1–2 seconds, in this short time they can cause all kinds of damage in the body, including taking hydrogen electrons from molecules in body tissues and damaging the tissues in the process. Antioxidants neutralize these free radicals by donating extra hydrogen electrons to them before they can take them from the body tissues. You should eat plenty of foods rich in antioxidants: vitamins A, C, E and betacarotene are the best known of these nutrients, although lycopene (found in tomatoes), zinc and manganese are also important. Many flavonoids (the chemicals that give bell peppers and fruits such as blueberries, blackberries, cherries and lemons their color) are also powerful antioxidants.

It is important that anyone with arthritis absorbs plenty of antioxidants, both by eating a diet rich in antioxidants and by taking a vitamin and mineral supplement. Ideally, these supplements should be taken under medical or nutritional supervision, so that they can be adapted to suit your particular needs.

VITAMIN A

Found in liver, especially fish liver oils, eggs, orange and yellow fruits, and green leafy vegetables, vitamin A should not be taken in excess, that is, in levels of over 10,000 IUs per day. A spoonful of that old favorite, cod liver oil, is the simple, if not the most pleasant, way of increasing Vitamin A intake. Alternatively, include chicken, calf's or lamb's liver in some dishes.

Left: Drinking too much tea and coffee may reduce the absorption of vital minerals, particularly iron. Naturally flavored fruit teas are a good substitute, and contain almost no calories.

A little chicken liver can be added to a meat stew without changing the flavor too much. However, as arthritis sufferers should be trying to reduce meat consumption, it is better to eat a fairly regular supply of eggs and eat plenty of yellow and orange vegetables (carrots, yellow, orange and red bell peppers, and yellow squash) and fruits in salads and vegetable dishes.

VITAMIN C

This is found in most fresh fruits and vegetables but is easily destroyed by the cooking process. Eating more fresh, raw fruits and vegetables automatically increases vitamin C consumption. People who are avoiding citrus fruits or members of the solanacae family (potatoes, bell peppers, chiles, tomatoes, eggplant) as part of an exclusion diet will still find an abundance of other fresh fruits and vegetables that contain substantial amounts of vitamin C.

VITAMIN E

This is found in most vegetable oils (olive and corn), nuts, seeds, avocados (which are also a rich source of vitamin C), peaches, broccoli, spinach and asparagus. The seeds and seed oils that are eaten as part of an anti-inflammatory diet will therefore have the additional benefit of providing a substantial amount of vitamin E.

SELENIUM

Grains and nuts are sources of selenium, but their precise content varies according to the soil in which they were grown. Selenium interacts with vitamin E, making both of these nutrients more powerful. Brazil nuts, grains and pulses (especially lentils), mung beans and red kidney beans are good for boosting the levels in the diet. Fish is also a good source of selenium.

BETACAROTENE

This is the best known of over 600 carotenoids, which are the plant

Above: Fruit is an excellent natural sweetener and can be used both fresh and dried. It also provides useful amounts of vitamin C and other trace elements.

Right: Supplements can ensure you receive the trace elements that may be missing, and are a useful source of antioxidants.

pigments that give yellow, orange and red fruits their color. Scientists are greatly interested in carotenoids, which they suspect may be even more powerful antioxidants than the established vitamins A, C and E. Like many of the carotenoids, betacarotene can be converted by the body into vitamin A. Betacarotene is to be found in carrots, apricots, cantaloupes, sweet potatoes, pumpkin, spinach, kale and parsley.

FOOD ALLERGIES

Although most conventional specialists dismiss food allergy as being a cause of arthritis, there is a growing body of evidence to suggest that it may be a trigger in a substantial number of cases of rheumatoid arthritis and, to a more limited extent, in other types of arthritis as well.

The amount of the food that is needed to trigger an allergic reaction, the strength of the reaction itself and the improvement that can be achieved by excluding the food from the diet, will all vary according to the individual. One sufferer's symptoms may disappear completely when they cut out the relevant food but return if they eat the smallest amount of the allergen. Another person may find that their condition improves to some extent if they cut down on a certain food, but it does not improve further if they cut the food out entirely. It is important that each person experiment with his or her own diet and is not distracted by the experiences of other people.

Of course, not everyone will find that changing their diet will cure, or even improve, their arthritis. However, most people will benefit from eating a healthier, balanced diet, and most arthritics, unless they are very slim, will probably benefit from losing some weight. Some arthritis sufferers (especially those with rheumatoid arthritis) may benefit to some extent by improving their diet.

POTENTIALLY ALLERGENIC FOODS

There is no food that is guaranteed not to cause an allergic reaction. Every food can provoke an allergy in someone, and it is perfectly possible that the allergy may show itself as arthritis. To complicate the issue, people can have an allergy to more than one food. So, to test properly for an allergic reaction, you need to try all foods, alone and together. Certain families of foods seem to be most frequently involved, however.

• Dairy products such as milk, cheese, cream, butter and yogurt.
• Vegetables from the deadly nightshade or solanacae family, such as red, green and yellow bell peppers, potatoes, tomatoes, tobacco, chiles and eggplant.
• Citrus fruits, especially orange juice.
• Wheat and all wheat derivatives.

CANDIDA
If candida (yeast overgrowth in your system) is a problem, then a two-pronged strategy is a good idea: treatment with anti-fungal medication and a diet excluding sugar and all fermented foods, to starve the yeast of nourishment.

Above, clockwise from top: Dairy products include: Cheddar cheese, cow's milk, yogurt made from cow's milk, Brie.

Above, clockwise from top: The solanacae family includes eggplant, red and green bell peppers, chiles, potatoes.

Above: Citrus fruits, and especially oranges and orange juice, can cause a severe allergic reaction in some people.

Above: Flour and pasta both contain wheat and should therefore be avoided by people following a wheat-free diet.

EXCLUSION DIETS

There is no guarantee that a food allergy has caused or worsened an individual case of arthritis; however, if it has, there could be substantial benefits in altering the diet to exclude those foods that trigger the arthritis. They include reduced pain, improved mobility, less joint deterioration, reduced use of drugs and fewer side effects. For a few people, the effects may be so positive as to amount to a cure. For most arthritics, excluding foods that their bodies cannot tolerate will not rid them of their arthritis, but it may improve their condition enough to be worth the effort of excluding those foods. Also, if a food upsets the body enough to aggravate arthritis, it may be damaging to your health in other respects, so that excluding it, or at least reducing the amount eaten, will probably be good for your general health.

Before embarking on an exclusion diet, a nutritionist and a physician should be consulted, especially for the very young or old, by pregnant women and by people on medication or who have health problems in addition to arthritis. A diet that excludes more than one group of foods (dairy products, citrus fruits, wheat and so on) should never be followed, except under medical supervision.

There are two methods of pinpointing a troublesome food: an allergy test and keeping a food diary.

ALLERGY TESTS

These vary in type and cost, from inexpensive tests offered by a few healthfood stores (which test for the basic six potential allergens) to a thorough blood analysis covering 100–200 foods and offering back-up information and advice. If you cannot face trying a strict exclusion diet for each of the possible groups of potentially allergenic foods, an allergy test may be a worthwhile shortcut. The result still has to be verified by excluding the food from the diet for a period of time.

However, be cautious when reading the test results. If a test records a reaction to a very large number of foods, the advice of a dietician or nutritionist should be taken before excluding them from the diet. More harm than good results from a starvation diet. If there is a genuine bad reaction to a number of foods, professional nutritional guidance must be taken to work through the problem and find a balanced solution.

KEEPING A FOOD DIARY

A food diary will cement the habit of really thinking about all foods that are eaten. It should be kept for a couple of weeks. Note everything eaten each day, from the marmalade licked off a spoon after breakfast to the bite taken from your child's sandwich. The diary must include notes on the arthritis condition—when it is worse or slightly better. There should be least five entries a day for both food and condition.

Above: It is a good idea to talk to your doctor or a nutritionist before embarking on an exclusion diet. He or she will be able to help you plan a diet so that you do not miss out on any essential food group.

DISCOVERING THE CULPRIT

After keeping a detailed food diary for a week or so, some kind of pattern may start to emerge. For example, do you always feel worse 30 minutes after a large glass of fresh orange juice for breakfast? The next step, and the only foolproof way to discover whether a food is having an adverse effect, is to exclude it from your diet for a period of at least one month. You will need to be patient when trying to pinpoint troublesome foods, as the process may take several months.

EMBARKING ON AN EXCLUSION DIET

The suspect food family is most likely one of the four usually associated with arthritis—dairy products, citrus fruit, wheat and the solanacae family of vegetables. The food that you suspect you may be allergic to must be rigorously excluded from the diet for at least two weeks, preferably one month. It takes a surprisingly long time for the food to work its way out of the body completely, and anyone genuinely sensitive to the food will react to the tiniest trace in the system.

It is relatively easy to exclude some foods from your diet, such as citrus fruits, as it is usually easy to identify them or dishes in which they have been used. It is far more difficult with the other three groups, however, as tomatoes, potatoes, dairy products and wheat products and their derivatives are used in almost every kind of ready-made food.

UNDERSTANDING LABELS

Although it is time-consuming, try to read every food label carefully to ensure that the product does not contain even a trace of the excluded food. To do this efficiently it is necessary to know all the names under which that product may appear on a label. For example, whey and casein are both constituents of milk, and modified starch is made from wheat.

FOODS TO AVOID

These lists show some of the products and ingredients that are not necessarily instantly identified as a source of the foods to be excluded. This is extensive enough to highlight the problem—many more individual items could be added.

WHEAT

Foods
Couscous
Curry powder
Farina
Instant hot beverages (such as coffee, tea, chocolate)
Semolina
Soy sauce (except wheat-free tamari)
White pepper in restaurants (can be adulterated with flour)

Ingredients
Cereal filler
Modified starch
Monosodium glutamate

Check labels of following:
Chinese sauces
Horseradish sauces
Ketchups
Mustards
Prepared meats
Salad dressings
Sauces
Sausages
Seasoning mixes
Soups
Candy

SOLANACAE

Eggplant
Bell peppers
Chile peppers
Potatoes
Tomatoes

Spices
Cayenne pepper
Chili powder
Curry powder
Paprika

DAIRY

Foods
Batter
Butter
Buttermilk
Cheese (including cream, ricotta and cottage cheeses)
Cream (heavy, whipping and light)
Créme fraîche
Ghee
Skim milk powder
Synthetic cream
Yogurt

Ingredients
Animal fats
Casein
Caseinates
Hydrolyzed casein or whey
Lactose
Milk solids
Nonfat milk solids
Whey
Whey protein or sugar

Check labels of following:
Chocolate
Low-fat spreads
Vegetable fats

CITRUS FRUIT

Clementines
Grapefruits
Lemons
Limes
Mandarins
Mineolas
Oranges
Satsumas
Tangerines
Ugli fruits

The number of ready-made dishes that are suitable for people following an exclusion diet is small, although there are a growing number of companies producing foods without dairy products, wheat or other individual ingredients.

ALTERNATIVE INGREDIENTS

It has become fairly easy to find alternatives to some of the basic ingredients that are commonly excluded.

Above: There is now a wide range of non-wheat flours, noodles and pastas.

WHEAT-FREE DIET

Although the number of companies making flour, breads, pastas, pizzas, cakes and cookies without wheat is increasing all the time, they are still relatively rare, and the products are comparatively expensive. Potato flour or cornstarch can be used for thickening soups, sauces and similar dishes, and bread, cakes and cookies can be made using wheat-free flours, chickpea flour or a combination of rice flour and ground oats.

DAIRY-FREE DIET

This means a diet free from cow's milk and all its products, not milk from sheep, goats or other animals.

Goat's, sheep's, soy or oat milk can be used instead of cow's milk in most savory dishes, and there are dozens of different soy milks to choose from. For sweet dishes, both rice milk and coconut milk are good alternatives. There are a number of dairy-free spreads (check the ingredients list carefully) that can be substituted for

Above: Soy milk and goat cheese are useful alternatives to dairy products.

butter, both on bread and when cooking or baking. There is also an increasing range of soy, sheep's milk and goat's milk yogurts and even ice creams. Cheese is a serious problem, as the food industry has still not managed to come up with a cheese substitute that tastes anything remotely like cheese, although there are a couple of soy "cheese" spreads that are perfectly fine.

Above: Introduce hearty root vegetables such as rutabaga, sweet potatoes and turnip.

Above: A thick stock can be used instead of tomatoes in many recipes.

SOLANACAE-FREE DIET

This diet excludes potatoes, tomatoes, peppers, chiles and eggplant. There are a number of root vegetables that can be used instead of potatoes in many recipes, such as sweet potatoes, celeriac, Jerusalem artichokes, parsnips, rutabagas and carrots; firm squashes are also a useful alternative.

Tomatoes are the most difficult item to replace in this family, as there is really no satisfactory substitute for their sweet, acidic flavor and their juice. Use lots of chopped onions and plenty of herbs with a little thick and well-flavored stock instead of tomatoes in recipes that rely on their juice.

Peppers, chiles and eggplant can be avoided fairly easily. The hot flavor of chile can be replaced by using black or white pepper. Remember that cayenne pepper is a form of ground dried chiles and paprika is made from peppers.

Above: Replace chiles with spices such as peppercorns, ground turmeric or ginger.

NO IMPROVEMENT?

A month on an exclusion diet may not yield any improvement in the arthritis. This may be because the wrong food group has been excluded. In that case, try again with another of the food groups. By working through all four of the food families, each will be eliminated in turn; it may be that this diet does not make any difference to the arthritis and that food group is genuinely not implicated in your case. Alternatively, the problem food may not have been located, or there could be more than one food causing the problem. There are a number of therapists who have had great success with specific diets that eliminate more than one type of food. For example, one therapist, himself an ex-arthritic, recommends a diet regime including only seafood, vegetables and rice.

PHYSICIAN-CONSULTED FOOD FASTS

If you have not had positive results after excluding the initial four food families, but still feel that food could be implicated, consult with your doctor about a food fast. On a four to five day fast, nothing but distilled water is consumed. If some food or drink is implicated, it will be excluded automatically during the fast, and there should be an improvement. If there is a beneficial result, serious food detective work has to be used to track down the food—or foods—that cause the problem. No one should embark on such a fast lightly. It should ONLY be done under the supervision of a doctor and when the person has time off from work, with nothing very much to do. This applies especially to those who are not in general good health, or are on medication. Apart from the fact that not eating for extended periods creates

Right: A food fast should only ever be undertaken when you have time on your hands because you may find yourself reacting badly and feeling very sick.

a feeling of light-headedness and results in headaches, anyone who reacts badly to certain foods may find that their body takes the opportunity to "detoxify" itself. This process can be quite dramatic and, like an alcoholic or a drug addict who is suddenly deprived of their addictive substance, the person can suddenly feel very sick.

USING FOOD TO CHALLENGE A POSITIVE RESULT

If the exclusion diet has produced positive results, and the arthritis has improved, if only a little, it has to be confirmed that it was the exclusion of that food that helped, not some other side-effect of the diet or a change in lifestyle. Therefore the body has to be "challenged" with the food.

Re-introduce the excluded food in a reasonable amount for one week. There may be an immediate reaction, or a far more gradual one after a few days. Either way, this confirms that the food is causing a problem. It is then up to the individual to decide whether the improvement in condition was worth the disruption to diet and daily life. It might be worth continuing your investigations into the diet to see whether other foods could be involved and whether further improvement may be possible if those foods are avoided.

A varied diet is always a good thing, and, as you continue to experiment with alternative ways of cooking and eating, you may even find yourself enjoying food more and regarding the experience as an adventure.

FOLLOWING A SPECIAL DIET

It is one thing knowing a theory, but quite another when it comes to putting it into practice, and this is particularly true of following a special diet. Try to be positive, focusing on different cooking methods and a variety of ingredients rather than on the foods to avoid.

A quick glance at all these recommendations might give you the impression that you will lose weight very fast, as there may seem to be very little left that you are allowed to eat. However, a diet adjusted to help ease arthritis can include just as much variety as a standard diet. It may take a little extra effort, but there is no reason why the changes should not be included in the family diet. As long as the changes are discreet, even fussy eaters will probably never notice. Adding new foods—especially when many of them are really tasty— is often easier than removing old favorites. In either case, involving the whole family makes cooking and eating easier and can turn meals into culinary adventures for everyone.

Browse through a few cookbooks from a range of different cultures for inspiration. Try traditional dishes from India, China, Malaysia and Indonesia, for example, and you will be amazed by the number of tasty dishes that are low in animal fats and high in the foods and nutrients you should be eating more of.

A FEW SIMPLE POINTS

• Use olive or sunflower oil for cooking rather than butter or lard.
• Try tofu or soy protein in a flavorful curry or stew instead of meat.
• Use soy, oat or rice milk in cooking rather than cow's milk.
• Cut down on chocolate, cakes and cookies, and increase your intake of fresh fruit.
• Add a few seeds or nuts to savory and sweet cooked dishes and to salads.
• Increase the number of raw vegetables that you eat.
• Try baking or steaming vegetables rather than frying or roasting them.

Above: A diet suitable for people with arthritis is low in fat and high in vitamins, and should be suitable for all members of the family. You will find it much easier to follow your diet if the rest of the family eats the same foods.

Right: Crushed pumpkin seeds can be used in a wide variety of dishes to increase your intake of GLAs. Try adding them to pastry or whole-wheat scones, sprinkling them on salads or stirring them into casseroles or risotto.

KITCHEN IMPROVEMENTS

With arthritis there is a good chance that your hands, and indeed the rest of your body, are not as agile or as mobile as they once were. Although we would hope that changing your diet improves the condition, it is also a good idea to look around the kitchen for anything that could be changed to make cooking easier.

If your hands are stiff or weak, if you use a cane, find it difficult to stand for long, or have trouble bending, there are a number of relatively minor alterations that can be made to kitchen units and large appliances to make your life easier. There are also a few special gadgets that are not too expensive and can make quite a difference.

CUPBOARDS

If opening cupboard doors is difficult, take the doors off, leaving open shelves or add curtains, which can be pulled open and shut easily. Consider taking shelves out of cupboards to make space for sitting at the counter with your knees underneath or to store a cart. If the work surfaces are too deep for you to reach the back wall comfortably, try adding a free-standing shallow storage shelf against the back wall. A rail along the front of the units provides extra support when getting around the kitchen and somewhere to hang a cane—as well as a dishtowel. Many people prefer to cook sitting down so, if the counters are too high, a small table can be ideal for sitting down to carry out some of the tasks involved in food preparation.

ELECTRICITY

Special switches can be installed (this means changing just the attachment) and you can buy plugs with handles for all appliances that are much easier to pull out of sockets.

TAPS

Lever taps are easier to operate than the regular type. If you do not want to change the taps, lever tap-turners can be put on existing taps.

STOVES AND MICROWAVES

A split-level stove with an eye-level oven is very useful for people who cannot bend. Even better, a combination microwave and convection oven is very accessible. Appliances with a special door opener will be easier to use for anyone with weak hands. A cheaper alternative for a small family is a small microwave and table-top burners and a toaster oven. All these plug into a standard socket and are easy to use and clean. Table-top burners get very hot, so care must be taken when using them. Electric frying pans are also useful, as they sit on a table. They can be used for boiling or stewing, and some food can be served right from the pan.

CARTS

A cart, ideally a fairly tall one, is invaluable in the kitchen for use as a table. It can also be pushed around as a walker/cart, and its handle provides a place for hanging a cane. Retail catalogs listing disabled equipment usually have a selection of reasonably priced, sturdy carts suitable for use in the kitchen.

Below: A small table can be ideal for chopping vegetables.

TONGS, KNIVES AND SCISSORS

A pair of long-handled tongs with insulated handles is invaluable for all kinds of tasks. Avoid using knives as much as possible, as it is all too easy to let them slip. Scissors can be used for many types of chopping jobs. Buy scissors with large chunky finger holes or that spring open automatically.

GRATERS, CAN OPENERS AND SCREWTOP OPENERS

Graters, especially the steady four-sided ones, are useful for many jobs. A plastic food mill, which grates by turning, is also handy. An electric can opener is the answer for those with stiff hands, but a manual opener with thick handles and an easy-to-grasp turning knob is less expensive. There are a selection of devices for removing tops from jars. Experiment at a kitchenware store to find one that you like.

Above: Plastic kitchenware is lighter than metal and therefore easier to lift.

BOWLS AND MEASURING CUPS

Look for kitchen equipment made from lightweight plastic. Replace any ceramic mixing bowls, glass measuring cups and metal colanders. If you are worried about the plastic bowl slipping when you are mixing, use a wet dish towel or a rubber mat (there are special mats for this purpose that are very good) to stop any movement.

Above: A pitcher holder bears the weight of the water and also makes pouring safer.

PITCHERS

A pitcher that can be filled through the spout and that is neither too heavy nor too difficult to lift is essential—always test it before buying. Kitchen holders, which save you from having to lift the appliance for pouring, are available.

HANDLES

Choose cutlery and equipment with big, thick handles. If you do not want to buy new items, you can buy large plastic handles that fit over existing ones. Less elegant, but equally effective for cutlery, is a piece of rubber tubing taped firmly in place. Some specialty cutlery has handles that can be bent. The user can move them into the position they find most comfortable.

Above: Cutlery with big, thick handles are easier to grip.

HELPING HANDS

A pair of magnetic pincers controlled by a lever on the end of a long handle is invaluable for picking up items when your reach is impaired. These are available at larger hardware and kitchen stores and specialty catalogs.

PROCESSORS, MIXERS AND BLENDERS

Small, hand-held appliances are easier to use than family-size models, most of which are heavy. Battery-powered cordless mixers are ideal.

Above: A cooking basket will keep you from having to lift a pan of boiling water.

SAUCEPANS

Iron casseroles may be wonderful for long, slow cooking, but they are hard for even able-bodied cooks to lift. Look for good-quality, light pans with long handles. The handles must be big and easy to grasp as well as being well insulated. Twin-handled pans are ideal for people with weak hands.

Chose a nonstick pan that will be easy to clean. Cooking in a nonstick pan requires less fat, another important consideration for arthritis sufferers.

A stainless steel cooking basket is a useful investment, as it allows you to remove and drain cooked vegetables without lifting a heavy pan of water. The pan can be emptied later when the water is cool.

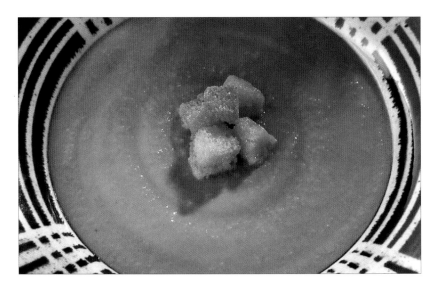

SOUPS AND APPETIZERS

Nutritious, easy to eat and easy to make, soups are excellent for

people with arthritis. They can be cooked in one pot, puréed with

a hand-held blender and drunk from a mug. Try one of these healthy

appetizers and boost your GLA intake with Green Mussels with

Cumin or Sizzling Salmon with Herbs. Remember that if your

hands are stiff it is easier—and safer—to chop herbs, bacon

and dried fruit with scissors than knives.

Fresh Pea Soup

This soup is a version of an old French recipe. Frozen peas are an excellent choice for those with arthritis: they are high in vitamin C and need no preparation.

INGREDIENTS

Serves 2
2 tablespoons oil
2–3 shallots, finely chopped or
  1 tablespoon dried onion
3 cups shelled fresh peas (from about
  3 pounds garden peas) or thawed
  frozen peas
2 cups water
3 tablespoons light cream, or omit if
  you are on a dairy-free diet
salt and ground black pepper
croutons or crumbled bacon,
  to garnish

1 Heat the oil in a flameproof casserole or saucepan. Add the shallots or dried onion and cook for about 3 minutes, stirring occasionally.

2 Add the peas and water. Cover the saucepan and let the mixture simmer for about 12 minutes if you are using young or frozen peas and up to 18 minutes for large or older peas, stirring occasionally.

—————— COOK'S TIP ——————

If your hands are stiff and painful, you can purée the soup in the pan with a hand-held blender and not strain it. The results won't be as smooth but will be just as tasty.

3 When the peas are tender, ladle them into a blender or food processor with a little of the cooking liquid and process, in batches if necessary, until the mixture is smooth.

4 Strain the soup through a fine sieve back into the casserole or saucepan. Stir in the cream, if using, and heat the soup through without boiling. Season with salt and freshly ground black pepper to taste and serve hot, garnished with croutons or bacon.

—————— NUTRITION NOTES ——————

Per portion:

Calories	309
Fat, total	17.2g
saturated fat	4.6g
Protein	13.1g
Carbohydrate	27.0g
sugar, total	11.4g
Fiber—NSP	11.3g
Sodium	30.6mg

Asparagus Soup with Crab

This soup has a subtle flavor that is bound to impress. Asparagus is a good source of vitamin E.

INGREDIENTS

Serves 6

3 pounds fresh asparagus
2 tablespoons olive oil
6¼ cups vegetable stock
2 tablespoons cornstarch
3 tablespoons light cream, or omit if
   you are on a dairy-free diet
salt and ground black pepper
6–7 ounces white crabmeat,
   to garnish

1 Trim the woody ends from the bottoms of the asparagus spears and cut the spears into 1-inch pieces. Use scissors if it is easier.

2 Heat the oil in a casserole or saucepan over medium-high heat. Add the asparagus and cook for 5–6 minutes, stirring frequently, until bright green, but not browned.

3 Add the stock and bring to a boil over high heat, skimming off any foam that rises to the surface. Simmer over medium heat for 3–5 minutes, until the asparagus is tender, yet crisp. Reserve 12–16 of the asparagus tips for garnishing. Season with salt and pepper, cover and continue cooking for 15–20 minutes, until very tender.

4 Purée the soup in a blender or food processor, or use a hand-held blender. Pour the soup back into the saucepan. Bring it back to a boil over medium-high heat.

5 Blend the cornstarch with about 3 tablespoons cold water and mix into the soup. Cook until thickened, then stir in the cream, if using. Season with salt and black pepper.

6 To serve, ladle the soup into bowls and top each with a spoonful of the crabmeat and a few of the reserved asparagus tips.

NUTRITION NOTES

Per portion:

Calories	165
Fat, total	7.2g
saturated fat	1.9g
Protein	13.4g
Carbohydrate	12.1g
sugar, total	4.5g
Fiber—NSP	3.7g
Sodium	583mg

COOK'S TIP

If you have difficulty lifting, use a hand-held blender in the pan. The soup will be chunkier, but will still taste as good.

Green Lentil Soup

This hearty North African soup is rich in the mineral selenium, an important antioxidant.

INGREDIENTS

Serves 4
1 cup green lentils
5 tablespoons olive oil
3 onions, finely chopped, or
   3 tablespoons dried onion
2 garlic cloves, thinly sliced, or
   2 teaspoons garlic purée
2 teaspoons cumin seeds, crushed
¼ teaspoon ground turmeric
2½ cups vegetable stock
salt and ground black pepper
2 tablespoons roughly chopped
   cilantro, to serve
warm bread, to serve

1 Put the lentils in a pan and cover with cold water. Bring to a boil and boil rapidly for 10 minutes; drain.

2 Heat 2 tablespoons of the oil in a deep saucepan and sauté two of the onions (or 2 tablespoons dried onion) with the garlic, cumin and turmeric for 3 minutes, stirring constantly.

3 Add the lentils and vegetable stock. Bring to a boil, then reduce the heat, cover and simmer gently for 30 minutes, until the lentils are soft.

4 Fry the third onion (or remaining 1 tablespoon dried onion) in the remaining oil until golden.

5 Use a potato masher to lightly mash the lentils and make the soup thick. Reheat gently and season with salt and ground black pepper to taste. Pour the soup into serving bowls. Stir the chopped cilantro into the fried onion and sprinkle on the soup to decorate. Serve immediately, with warm bread.

COOK'S TIPS

• If you have difficulty lifting heavy pans, remove the lentils from their boiling water into the soup pot with a slotted spoon or ladle. If the lentils are really well cooked they will barely need mashing.
• If you prefer to use fresh onion and garlic, you can use an onion chopper to save you slicing them.

NUTRITION NOTES

Per portion:

Calories	320
Fat, total	15.0g
saturated fat	2.0g
Protein	15.7g
Carbohydrate	32.6g
sugar, total	4.0g
Fiber—NSP	5.8g
Sodium	369mg

Spanish Garlic Soup

Topped with toasted French bread, this delicious and satisfying soup is almost a meal in itself. Try serving it for a winter lunch and let its wonderful aroma bring you a little Mediterranean sunshine.

INGREDIENTS

Serves 4

2 tablespoons olive oil
4 large garlic cloves, peeled
4 slices French bread, ¼ inch thick, or if you are on a wheat-free diet, leave the bread out and have the soup just with the egg
1 tablespoon paprika or, if you are on a solanacae-free diet, ground ginger
4 cups vegetable stock
¼ teaspoon ground cumin
pinch of saffron threads
4 eggs
salt and ground black pepper
chopped fresh parsley, to garnish

1 Preheat the oven to 450°F. Heat the oil gently in a large pan. Add the whole garlic cloves and cook until golden. Remove and set aside. Toast the bread in the oven until it is golden.

2 Add the paprika or ground ginger to the pan, and fry for a few seconds. Stir in the stock, cumin and saffron. Crush the reserved garlic cloves and add to the pan. Season with salt and pepper, and cook for about 5 minutes.

3 Ladle into four ovenproof bowls and break an egg into each. Place a slice of bread on each egg and bake for 3–4 minutes, until the eggs are set. Garnish with parsley; serve.

--- COOK'S TIPS ---

• To prevent the oil from overheating, add a tablespoon of water when frying the garlic.
• If you find it difficult to put the soup bowls into the oven, you can either omit the eggs and serve the soup just with the bread and garlic, or poach the eggs in the soup and merely ladle them out with the soup.

--- NUTRITION NOTES ---

Per portion:

Calories	249
Fat, total	12.8g
saturated fat	2.7g
Protein	12.3g
Carbohydrate	22.5g
sugar, total	0.8g
Fiber—NSP	0.6g
Sodium	668mg

Sorrel, Spinach and Salmon Soup

This is an excellent cold, Russian summer soup. It is traditionally made with *kvas*, a beer made from wheat, rye and buckwheat, but cider works equally well.

INGREDIENTS

Serves 4
2 tablespoons olive oil
8 ounces sorrel, washed and
    stems removed
8 ounces young spinach, washed and
    stems removed
1 ounce fresh horseradish, grated or
    1 tablespoon grated horseradish in a jar
3 cups cider
1 pickled cucumber, finely chopped
    or grated
2 tablespoons chopped fresh dill, plus
    extra sprigs to garnish
8 ounces cooked salmon, skinned
    and boned
salt and ground black pepper

1 Heat the oil in a large pan. Add the sorrel and spinach leaves and the horseradish. Cover and cook gently for 3–4 minutes or until the sorrel and spinach leaves are wilted.

--- COOK'S TIP ---

If sorrel is unavailable, use double the amount of spinach instead and, just before serving, add a dash of lemon juice to the soup. Use vinegar if you are on a citrus-free diet.

2 Spoon the cooked leaves into a food processor and process into a fine purée, or purée with a hand-held processor. Ladle into a tureen or bowl and stir in the cider, pickled cucumber and chopped dill.

3 Chop the salmon into even, bite-size pieces. Add them to the soup, then season with plenty of salt and pepper to taste. Chill the soup for at least 3 hours before serving, garnished with a sprig of dill.

--- NUTRITION NOTES ---

Per portion:

Calories	246
Fat, total	12.6g
saturated fat	1.9g
Protein	14.5g
Carbohydrate	6.6g
sugar, total	6.5g
Fiber—NSP	2.3g
Sodium	195mg

Carrot and Cilantro Soup

Carrots and cilantro are often combined in soups, as their flavors are so complementary. This version uses soy milk, making it particularly suitable for people on a dairy-free diet.

INGREDIENTS

Serves 4

1 pound carrots, preferably young
  and tender
3 tablespoons sunflower oil
1 onion, chopped or 2 tablespoons
  dried onion
1 celery stalk, sliced plus 2–3 pale leafy
  celery tops
2 small potatoes or, if you are on a
  solanacae-free diet, 1 sweet potato,
  peeled and cubed
4 cups chicken stock
2–3 teaspoons ground cilantro
1 tablespoon chopped cilantro
scant 1 cup soy milk
salt and ground black pepper

1 Trim the carrots, peel if necessary and cut into chunks. Heat 2 tablespoons of the sunflower oil in a large pan and cook the onion over low heat for 3–4 minutes, until softened.

2 Add the sliced celery and potatoes or sweet potato to the onion in the saucepan, cook for a few minutes and then add the carrots. Cook the vegetables over low heat for 3–4 minutes, stirring frequently, and then cover. Reduce the heat even further and sweat for about 10 minutes. Stir occasionally so the vegetables do not stick to the bottom of the pan.

3 Add the stock, bring to a boil and then partially cover and simmer for another 8–10 minutes until the carrots and potatoes are tender.

4 Remove 6–8 tiny celery leaves for garnish and finely chop the remaining leaves (about 1 tablespoon once chopped). Heat the remaining oil in a pan and fry the ground cilantro for about 1 minute, stirring constantly.

5 Reduce the heat and add the cilantro and celery leaves. Cook for about 1 minute. Set aside.

6 Process the soup in a food processor or blender or with a hand-held blender and pour back into the saucepan. Stir in the soy milk, cilantro mixture and seasoning. Heat gently, taste and adjust the seasoning. Serve garnished with the reserved celery leaves.

COOK'S TIP

If you have difficulty with your hands you can leave the carrots, potato and celery whole and unpeeled—just make sure you wash them well. They will be much easier to cut up when cooked and soft. Alternatively, you could use dried vegetables.

NUTRITION NOTES

Per portion:

Calories	182
Fat, total	9.8g
saturated fat	1.3g
Protein	5.1g
Carbohydrate	19.3g
sugar, total	11.1g
Fiber—NSP	3.8g
Sodium	515mg

Dolmades

This tasty Greek dish of stuffed grape leaves has become a classic.

INGREDIENTS

Makes 24

28 fresh young grape leaves, soaked, or
    leaves from a package or can
2 tablespoons olive oil
1 large onion, finely chopped, or
    2 tablespoons dried onion
1 teaspoon garlic purée
2 cups cooked long-grain rice, or
    mixed white and wild rice
about 3 tablespoons pine nuts
1 tablespoon sliced almonds
¼ cup golden raisins
1 tablespoon snipped fresh chives
1 tablespoon finely chopped fresh mint
juice of ½ lemon or, if you are on a
    citrus-free diet, 1 tablespoon white
    wine vinegar
⅔ cup white wine
hot vegetable stock
salt and ground black pepper
fresh mint sprig, to garnish
plain organic yogurt and pita bread, to
    serve (omit if you are on a dairy- or
    wheat-free diet)

1 If you are using fresh grape leaves, bring a pan of water to a boil and cook the grape leaves for 2–3 minutes. They will darken after about 1 minute, and simmering for another minute or so will ensure that they are pliable.

2 If using leaves from a package or can, place them in a large bowl, cover with boiling water and let sit for a few minutes until the leaves can easily be separated. Rinse them under cold water and drain on paper towels.

3 Heat the oil in a small frying pan and sauté the onion and garlic gently for 3–4 minutes, until soft. Spoon into a large bowl and add the cooked rice.

4 Stir in 2 tablespoons of the pine nuts, the almonds, golden raisins, chives and mint. Squeeze in the lemon juice or vinegar. Season to taste and mix well.

5 Set aside four large grape leaves. Lay a grape leaf on a clean work surface, veined-side facing up. Place a spoonful of filling near the stem, fold the lower part of the grape leaf over it and roll up, folding in the sides as you go. Stuff the rest in the same way.

6 Line the bottom of a deep frying pan or flameproof casserole dish with the reserved grape leaves. Place the dolmades close together in the pan, seam-side down, in a single layer. Pour in the wine and enough stock to just cover. Anchor the dolmades by placing a plate on top of them, then cover the pan and simmer gently for 30 minutes.

7 Transfer the dolmades to a plate. Cool, chill, then garnish with the remaining pine nuts and the mint. Serve with a little yogurt and pita bread, if desired.

NUTRITION NOTES	
Per portion:	
Calories	69
Fat, total	2.9g
saturated fat	0.3g
Protein	1.4g
Carbohydrate	10.1g
sugar, total	1.8g
Fiber—NSP	0.3g
Sodium	70mg

Green Mussels with Cumin

Many people with osteoarthritis take green mussel supplements to help manage their condition—so this dish is not only delicious but excellent for your joints.

INGREDIENTS

Serves 4

3 tablespoons fresh parsley
3 tablespoons cilantro
1 garlic clove, crushed
pinch of ground cumin
2 tablespoons unsalted butter, or, if you are on a dairy-free diet, substitute 2 tablespoons olive oil
¼ cup brown bread crumbs, or, if you are on a wheat-free diet, substitute 3 tablespoons crushed plain potato chips
ground black pepper
12 green mussels or 24 small mussels on the half-shell
fresh parsley leaves, to garnish

1 Chop the herbs finely. Use a broad-handled herb chopper or scissors if you find it easier.

NUTRITION NOTES

Per portion:

Calories	84
Fat, total	6.1g
saturated fat	3.8g
Protein	2.4g
Carbohydrate	5.3g
sugar, total	0.3g
Fiber—NSP	0.0g
Sodium	115mg

2 Beat the garlic, herbs, cumin and butter or oil together with a wooden spoon, or purée them together in a small food processor or coffee grinder.

3 Stir in the bread crumbs or chips and the ground black pepper.

4 Carefully spoon a little of the mixture for the topping on to each mussel and cook under a medium-hot grill for 2 minutes. Serve the mussels immediately, garnished with the fresh parsley leaves.

Whiting Fillets with Polenta Crust

Whiting is a flaky, white fish with a delicate flavor, which the crisp polenta coating helps to seal in.

INGREDIENTS

Serves 4

8 small whiting fillets
finely grated zest of 1 lemon, or omit if on a citrus-free diet
2 cups polenta
3 tablespoons olive oil
salt and ground black pepper

To serve

2 tablespoons chopped mixed fresh herbs such as parsley, chervil and chives, plus extra whole leaves
steamed spinach
red onion, sliced
toasted pine nuts

— COOK'S TIPS —

• Use quick-cooking polenta if you can, as it will make a better crunchy coating.
• If your hands are stiff, it may be easier to use scissors to chop the herbs.

1 Make four small cuts in each fillet to stop the fish from curling up when it is cooked.

— NUTRITION NOTES —

Per portion:

Calories	435
Fat, total	10.6g
saturated fat	1.4g
Protein	40.6g
Carbohydrate	42.4g
sugar, total	0.0g
Fiber—NSP	0.0g
Sodium	191mg

2 Season and, if using lemon zest, sprinkle most of it on the fish.

3 Press the polenta onto the fillets. Chill for 30 minutes.

4 Heat the oil in a frying pan and fry the fillets for 3–4 minutes on each side. Garnish with the chopped herbs and herb leaves, and the reserved lemon zest. Serve with steamed spinach, sliced red onion and toasted pine nuts.

Sizzling Salmon with Herbs

Salmon is well known to arthritis sufferers for its anti-inflammatory properties. This is an unusual and exciting way to serve fresh salmon. A simple green salad makes a good side dish.

INGREDIENTS

Serves 4

4 salmon steaks, 6–7 ounces each
2 tablespoons olive oil
3 tablespoons chopped fresh ginger
   root or 2 tablespoons ground ginger
   or 3 tablespoons ginger purée
6 tablespoons chopped scallions
6 tablespoons chopped cilantro
2 fluid ounces soy sauce, which should
   be wheat-free tamari if you are on a
   wheat-free diet, plus extra to serve
salt and ground black pepper
cilantro sprigs, to garnish

1 Bring some water to a boil in the bottom of a steamer.

2 Season the fish steaks on both sides with salt and pepper.

NUTRITION NOTES

Per portion:

Calories	421
Fat, total	27.5g
saturated fat	4.6g
Protein	41.9g
Carbohydrate	1.5g
sugar, total	0.3g
Fiber—NSP	0.1g
Sodium	948mg

3 Place the fish steaks in the top part of the steamer. Cover the pan and steam the fish for 7–8 minutes or until it is opaque all the way through.

4 Heat the oil and gently cook the ginger root, or ginger powder or purée, with the scallions.

5 Place the salmon on warmed plates. Divide the chopped cilantro among the salmon steaks. Spoon on the ginger and the scallions. Drizzle 1 tablespoon soy sauce on each salmon steak and serve with small bowls of extra soy sauce alongside. Garnish with cilantro sprigs.

SALADS AND SIDE DISHES

A great selection of light dishes are included here, all of which are easy to

make and full of nutrients to help alleviate your arthritis.

Pasta salads are filling and tasty, and can include salmon or seeds to boost

your intake of inflammation-reducing GLAs and ALAs. Lentils are

a good choice when you are cutting down on meat consumption: try

the substantial Egyptian Rice with Lentils and the traditional Indian

Dhal with Tadka.

Smoked Salmon, Coconut and Dill Pasta

The coconut milk gives this dish an unusual flavor.

INGREDIENTS

Serves 4

3 cups pasta twists, wheat-free if you
   are on a wheat-free diet
6 large sprigs fresh dill, chopped, plus
   more sprigs to garnish
2 tablespoons extra virgin olive oil
1 tablespoon white wine vinegar
1¼ cups coconut milk
6 ounces smoked salmon
salt and ground black pepper

1 Boil the pasta until just cooked.
Drain and rinse under cold water.

2 Make the dressing by combining all
the remaining ingredients, apart
from the smoked salmon and the dill
for the garnish, in the bowl of a food
processor. Alternatively, use a hand-
held blender in a bowl and blend well.

3 Slice the salmon into small strips
with scissors. Place the cooled pasta
and the smoked salmon in a serving
bowl. Pour on the dressing and toss
carefully. Garnish with the dill sprigs.

NUTRITION NOTES	
Per portion:	
Calories	678
Fat, total	35.0g
saturated fat	23.8g
Protein	24.6g
Carbohydrate	70.5g
sugar, total	6.3g
Fiber—NSP	2.7g
Sodium	632mg

Avocado and Pasta Salad with Cilantro

INGREDIENTS

Serves 4

3¾ cups chicken stock
2 cups pasta bows, wheat-free if you are
   on a wheat-free diet
4 celery stalks, finely chopped
2 avocados, peeled and chopped
1 garlic clove, peeled and chopped, or
   ½ teaspoon garlic purée
½ cup aged Cheddar cheese, grated, or
   omit if you are on a dairy-free diet
1 tablespoon chopped cilantro, plus
   some whole leaves to garnish
2 tablespoons toasted sunflower seeds

For the dressing
⅔ cup extra virgin olive oil (cold
   pressed is best)
1 tablespoon cider vinegar
2 tablespoons lemon juice and grated
   zest of 1 lemon, or if you are on a
   citrus-free diet, use 3 tablespoons
   vinegar and omit the zest
1 teaspoon Dijon mustard
1 tablespoon chopped cilantro
salt and ground black pepper

1 Bring the stock to a boil, add the
pasta, and simmer for 10 minutes,
until cooked. Drain; set aside to cool.

2 Mix the celery, avocados, garlic,
cheese and cilantro in a bowl and
add the cooled pasta. Sprinkle on the
sunflower seeds.

3 To make the dressing, place all the
ingredients in a food processor or
coffee grinder and process until the
cilantro is very finely chopped.
Alternatively, use a hand-held blender
in a bowl and blend well. Serve the
dressing separately, or pour onto the
salad and toss before serving. Garnish
with cilantro leaves.

NUTRITION NOTES	
Per portion:	
Calories	303
Fat, total	13.9g
saturated fat	2.4g
Protein	10.2g
Carbohydrate	36.5g
sugar, total	1.6g
Fiber—NSP	3.7g
Sodium	643mg

Red Rice Salad Niçoise

The sweet, nutty flavor of red rice makes a delicious variation on a classic Salad Niçoise. The thick steaks of fresh tuna make this tasty salad substantial enough to be a meal in its own right.

INGREDIENTS

Serves 6

1½ pounds fresh tuna, sliced into
    ¾-inch thick steaks
1¾ cups Camargue red rice
fish or vegetable stock or water
1 pound green beans
1 pound frozen and cooked or drained,
    canned fava beans
1 Romaine lettuce
1 pound tiny cherry tomatoes or, if you
    are on a solanacae-free diet, omit and
    double the amount of olives
2 tablespoons cilantro, chopped
3 hard-boiled eggs (optional)
1½ cups pitted black olives
olive oil, for brushing

For the marinade
1 onion, peeled and roughly chopped,
    or 2 tablespoons dried onion
2 garlic cloves, peeled or 2 heaping
    teaspoons garlic purée
½ bunch fresh parsley
½ bunch cilantro
2 teaspoons paprika, or omit if you are
    on a solanacae-free diet
3 tablespoons olive oil
3 tablespoons water
2 tablespoons white wine vinegar
1 tablespoon fresh lime or lemon juice
    or, if you are on a citrus-free diet,
    3 tablespoons cider vinegar
salt and ground black pepper

For the dressing
2 tablespoons fresh lime or lemon
    juice or, if you are on a citrus-free
    diet, cider vinegar
1 teaspoon Dijon mustard
½ garlic clove, crushed or ¼ teaspoon
    garlic purée (optional)
¼ cup olive oil
¼ cup sunflower oil

1 First, make the marinade for the tuna steaks. Place all the ingredients for the marinade in a blender or food processor and process for 30–40 seconds, until all of the vegetables and herbs are finely chopped.

2 Prick the tuna steaks all over with a fork, then lay them side by side in a shallow dish. Spoon on the marinade, turning the fish to coat each piece thoroughly.

3 Cover the dish with plastic wrap and let the tuna steaks marinate in a cool place for 2–4 hours.

─── NUTRITION NOTES ───	
Per portion:	
Calories	638
Fat, total	39.7g
saturated fat	27.1g
Protein	4.3g
Carbohydrate	58g
sugar, total	4.8g
Fiber—NSP	7.5g
Sodium	937mg

4 Cook the rice in the stock or water, following the instructions on the package. Drain; set aside to cool.

5 To make the dressing, mix the citrus juice or cider vinegar, mustard and garlic, if using, in a bowl. Whisk in the oils, then add salt and pepper to taste. Stir ¼ cup of the dressing into the rice, then spoon the rice into a large serving dish.

6 Steam the green beans until tender. Mix the green and fava beans into the rice. Discard the outer leaves from the lettuce and tear the inner leaves into pieces. Add to the salad with the tomatoes, if using, and cilantro. Shell the hard-boiled eggs, if using, and cut them into sixths. Preheat the broiler.

7 Arrange the tuna steaks on the broiler pan. Brush with the marinade and a little olive oil. Broil for 3–4 minutes on each side, until the fish is tender and flakes easily when tested with the tip of a sharp knife. Brush with marinade and more oil when turning the fish over.

8 Let the fish cool a little, then break it into large pieces. Toss into the salad with the olives and the remaining dressing. Decorate the salad with the eggs, if using, and serve.

─── VARIATION ───

This dish works well with swordfish steaks if tuna fish steaks aren't readily available.

Mixed Herb Salad with Toasted Seeds

A delicious light salad sprinkled with seeds packed with GLAs, the acid that contains anti-inflammatory agents helpful to arthritis sufferers. It is a wonderfully simple salad, and is the perfect side dish to a rich, heavy meal, as it contains fresh herbs that aid digestion.

INGREDIENTS

Serves 4

4 cups mixed salad leaves
2 cups mixed salad herbs, such as cilantro, parsley and basil
3 tablespoons pumpkin seeds
3 tablespoons sunflower seeds

For the dressing
¼ cup extra virgin olive oil
1 tablespoon balsamic vinegar
½ teaspoon Dijon mustard
salt and ground black pepper

1 To make the dressing, whisk the ingredients with a fork in a small bowl, or place in a screw-top jar and shake until combined.

--- HEALTH BENEFITS ---

• Fresh parsley is high in vitamin C and iron.
• Pumpkin seeds and sunflower seeds, although high in calories, are packed full of vitamins and minerals, including vitamin E, iron and zinc.

2 Put the salad and herb leaves in a large bowl.

3 Toast the pumpkin and sunflower seeds in a dry frying pan over medium heat or under the broiler for about 2 minutes or until golden, tossing frequently to prevent them from burning. Let the seeds cool slightly before sprinkling them on the salad.

4 Pour the dressing onto the salad and toss with your hands until the leaves are well coated, then serve.

--- COOK'S TIP ---

Balsamic vinegar adds an intensely rich, sweet taste to the dressing, but if it is not available, red or white wine vinegar could be used instead.

--- NUTRITION NOTES ---

Per portion:

Calories	178
Fat, total	17.0g
saturated fat	2.3g
Protein	3.3g
Carbohydrate	2.8g
sugar, total	0.8g
Fiber—NSP	1.5g
Sodium	6.1mg

Baked Fennel with a Crumb Crust

The delicate aniseed flavor of baked fennel goes well with tomatoes. Serve it with ratatouille or, if you are on a solanacae-free diet, with risotto. Fennel contains betacarotene, which the body converts into vitamin A.

INGREDIENTS

Serves 4

3 fennel bulbs, cut lengthwise
   into quarters
2 tablespoons olive oil
1 garlic clove, chopped or
   1 teaspoon garlic purée
½ cup day-old whole-wheat bread
   crumbs or, if you are on a wheat-free
   diet, 2 small packages of plain potato
   chips; crushed
2 tablespoons chopped fresh
   flat-leaf parsley
salt and ground black pepper
fennel fronds, to garnish (optional)

COOK'S TIP

If you have difficulty using your hands, cook the fennel whole in the boiling water, remove with a slotted spoon and quarter when cooked, as it will be easier to cut.

1 Cook the fennel in a saucepan of boiling salted water for 10 minutes or until just tender.

2 Drain the fennel and place in a baking dish or roasting pan, then brush lightly with half of the olive oil. Meanwhile, preheat the oven to 375°F.

3 In a large mixing bowl, stir the garlic, bread crumbs or crushed chips and parsley together with the rest of the olive oil. Sprinkle the topping evenly on the fennel, then season well with salt and pepper.

4 Bake for 30 minutes, until the crust is crisp and the fennel tender. Serve hot, garnished with a few fennel fronds.

NUTRITION NOTES

Per portion:

Calories	120
Fat, total	6.1g
saturated fat	0.8g
Protein	3.4g
Carbohydrate	13.7g
sugar, total	9.5g
Fiber—NSP	5.6g
Sodium	119mg

Carter's Millet

This dish was originally cooked over an open fire by carters who traveled across the steppes of southern Ukraine. It is a filling dish for a chilly day.

INGREDIENTS

Serves 4

scant 1¼ cups millet
2½ cups vegetable stock
4 ounces bacon with the rind removed, chopped
1 tablespoon olive oil
1 small onion, chopped or 1½ teaspoons dried onion
3 cups sliced or chopped small field mushrooms
1 tablespoon chopped fresh mint
salt and ground black pepper

1 Rinse the millet in a sieve under cold running water. Put in a pan with the stock, bring to a boil and simmer, covered, for 30 minutes, until the stock has been absorbed.

2 Dry-fry the bacon in a nonstick pan for 5 minutes or until brown and crisp. Remove and set aside.

3 Add the oil to the pan and cook the onion and mushrooms for 10 minutes, until starting to brown.

4 Add the cooked bacon, onion and mushrooms to the millet. Stir in the mint and season with salt and pepper. Heat gently for 1–2 minutes before serving.

COOK'S TIPS

The millet could be cooked in an electric frying pan and the other ingredients added as they are ready. The dish can then be served from the pan. If fresh mint is not readily available, use flat-leaf parsley or cilantro. Chop the bacon with scissors if you find this easier.

NUTRITION NOTES

Per portion:

Calories	332
Fat, total	10.9g
saturated fat	2.8g
Protein	10.6g
Carbohydrate	46.0g
sugar, total	0.5g
Fiber—NSP	1.1g
Sodium	738mg

Egyptian Rice with Lentils

This is a simple, highly nutritious and very filling dish. It can be served as a side dish or simply enjoyed as a meal in itself.

INGREDIENTS

Serves 6

1½ cups large brown lentils, soaked overnight in water
2 large onions or ¼ cup dried onion
3 tablespoons olive oil
1 tablespoon ground cumin
½ teaspoon ground cinnamon
generous 1 cup long-grain rice
salt and ground black pepper
flat-leaf parsley, to garnish

1 Drain the lentils and put them in the top of a steamer. Put enough water in the bottom of the steamer to cover the lentils by 2 inches.

2 Bring the water to a boil, cover the pan and simmer for 40 minutes to 1½ hours or until the lentils are tender. Remove the top of the steamer with the lentils and drain.

3 Slice one of the onions very finely. Chop the other onion. Heat 1 tablespoon of the olive oil in a saucepan, add the chopped onion and sauté until soft.

4 Add the drained lentils to the pan. Season with salt and pepper, then add the cumin and cinnamon.

5 Measure the volume of rice and add it, with the same volume of water, to the lentil mixture. Cover the saucepan and simmer for about 20 minutes or until the rice is tender.

6 Heat the remaining olive oil in a frying pan, and cook the sliced onion until very dark brown.

--- COOK'S TIPS ---

• If you would find it difficult to slice the onion for the topping, chop both onions as finely as you can.
• Cook the chopped onion in an electric frying pan, then add the lentils and rice. The dish can then be served from the pan.

7 Transfer the rice and lentil mixture to a serving bowl and sprinkle the fried onion on top. Garnish with flat-leaf parsley. This dish can be served hot or cold.

--- NUTRITION NOTES ---

Per portion:

Calories	380
Fat, total	8.0g
saturated fat	1.2g
Protein	17.4g
Carbohydrate	63.8g
sugar, total	2.9g
Fiber—NSP	5.9g
Sodium	9.7mg

Dhal with Tadka

Serve this aromatic Indian dish with naan or a wheat-free bread, if desired, to mop up the delicious sauce.

INGREDIENTS

Serves 4

3 tablespoons olive or sunflower oil
2 teaspoons black mustard seeds
1 onion, finely chopped or
 2 teaspoons dried onion
2 garlic cloves, finely chopped or
 2 teaspoons garlic purée
1 teaspoon ground turmeric
1 teaspoon ground cumin
2 fresh green chiles, seeded and finely chopped or, if you are on a solanacae-free diet, 2-ounce piece of ginger root, peeled and finely chopped, or 2 teaspoons powdered ginger
1 cup red lentils
1¼ cups canned coconut milk
1 batch tadka (see Cook's Tip)
cilantro sprigs, to garnish

1 Heat the oil in a large saucepan or frying pan. Add the mustard seeds. When they start to pop, add the onion and garlic and cook for 5–10 minutes, until soft.

VARIATION

This dish is also excellent made with yellow split peas. Like lentils, split peas do not hold their shape when cooked, making them perfect for dhals.

NUTRITION NOTES

Per portion:

Calories	258
Fat, total	6.5g
saturated fat	1.0g
Protein	14.0g
Carbohydrate	38.3g
sugar, total	7.1g
Fiber—NSP	3.3g
Sodium	103.8mg

2 Stir in the turmeric, cumin and chiles or ginger and cook for 2 minutes. Add the lentils with 4 cups water and the coconut milk and bring to a boil.

3 Cover the saucepan and simmer for about 40 minutes, adding water if necessary. The lentils should be soft and should have absorbed most of the liquid. Transfer the dhal to a serving dish and keep warm.

4 Follow the instructions in the Cook's Tip to prepare the tadka, then pour onto the dhal. Garnish with cilantro sprigs and serve immediately.

COOK'S TIP

A tadka is a mixture of spices and flavorings fried in mustard oil to release their flavors, then added to Indian dishes such as dhal or vegetables.

INGREDIENTS

¼ cup mustard oil
3–4 tablespoons cumin seeds
1 small onion, finely chopped
¼ cup finely chopped cilantro

1 Heat the mustard oil until it is just smoking, then turn off the heat and let the oil cool briefly.

2 Reheat the oil and fry the cumin seeds until they change color. Add the onion and cook until it turns golden.

3 Finally, add the cilantro and stir for a few seconds, then pour the mixture onto the dhal.

Mashed Sweet Potatoes with Garlic

Orange-fleshed sweet potatoes are delicious mashed with garlic-flavored olive or walnut oil. Sweet potatoes are packed with vitamins too. They are not members of the potato family, so they are ideal if you are on a solanacae-free diet.

INGREDIENTS

Serves 4

4 large sweet potatoes, peeled, total weight about 2 pounds, cubed
3 tablespoons walnut or olive oil
3 garlic cloves, crushed or 2 teaspoons garlic purée
salt and ground black pepper

1 Place the sweet potatoes in a saucepan containing boiling water and cook for about 15 minutes or until tender. Cook them in the top half of a steamer if that is easier.

2 Heat the oil in a saucepan, then sauté the garlic over low to medium heat for 1–2 minutes, until light golden, stirring to prevent the garlic from burning.

3 Pour the garlic oil onto the sweet potatoes and season with salt and plenty of black pepper. Mash thoroughly until smooth and creamy. Serve immediately while the potatoes are piping hot.

NUTRITION NOTES

Per portion:

Calories	269
Fat, total	8.9g
saturated fat	1.4g
Protein	2.7g
Carbohydrate	47.9g
sugar, total	12.8g
Fiber—NSP	5.4g
Sodium	90.0mg

COOK'S TIPS

• Sweet potatoes have tough skins, so they do need to be peeled. If you find this difficult, cook them first and peel them once cooked—it is easier.
• If the potatoes seem dry when you are mashing them, add a little milk.
• If you have difficulty mashing by hand, you can use a hand-held blender. .

Warm Leeks with Vinaigrette

Use tender baby leeks for this dish if you can find them, and unless you are on a wheat-free diet, mop up the vinaigrette with thick chunks of crusty bread.

INGREDIENTS

Serves 6

12 small leeks (total weight about
  3 pounds)
2 eggs, hard-boiled
1 tablespoon Dijon mustard
2 tablespoons lemon juice or, if you are
  on a citrus-free diet, white wine vinegar
6 tablespoons sunflower oil
6 tablespoons extra virgin olive oil, plus
  more if needed
salt and ground black pepper
1–2 tablespoons snipped fresh chives,
  to garnish

1 Remove the dark tough outer leaves of the leeks, then cut all the leeks to the same length, and trim the dark green tops.

2 Trim the root ends, leaving enough to hold the leeks together, then split the top half of the leeks lengthwise and rinse well under cold running water.

3 Lay the leeks flat in a large frying pan, pour in enough boiling water to just cover them and add a little salt. Cook the leeks over medium-high heat for 7–10 minutes, until just tender. Carefully remove the leeks with a slotted spoon, then lay them on a dish towel and press them gently to remove as much liquid as possible.

4 In a bowl, mash together the hard-boiled egg yolks and mustard to form a smooth paste. Season and add the lemon juice or vinegar, stirring until smooth. Slowly whisk in the sunflower oil, followed by the olive oil to make a thick, creamy vinaigrette. You can also whisk the vinaigrette together in a food processor, or in a bowl with a hand-held blender.

5 Arrange the leeks in a serving dish and pour on the vinaigrette while the leeks are still warm. Chop the egg whites and sprinkle them on the leeks, then sprinkle on the snipped fresh chives and serve warm or at room temperature.

NUTRITION NOTES	
Per portion:	
Calories	272
Fat, total	25.1g
saturated fat	3.6g
Protein	5.8g
Carbohydrate	6.2g
sugar, total	4.7g
Fiber—NSP	4.7g
Sodium	30.9mg

Braised Red Cabbage

This dish is a wonderful deep-red color and has a rich and sweet flavor.

INGREDIENTS

Serves 8

2 tablespoons vegetable oil
2 medium onions, thinly sliced
  or chopped or 3 tablespoons
  dried onion
2 apples, peeled, cored and thinly
  sliced or, if peeling the apples is
  difficult, leave the skins on and
  chop them roughly
1 head red cabbage (about
  2–2½ pounds), trimmed, cored,
  halved and thinly sliced
¼ cup red wine vinegar
1–2 tablespoons sugar
¼ teaspoon ground cloves
1–2 teaspoons mustard seeds
⅓ cup raisins or currants
about ½ cup red wine or water
1–2 tablespoons red currant jelly
  (optional)
salt and ground black pepper

1 Heat the oil over medium heat. Add the onions and cook for 7–10 minutes, until they are golden.

2 Add the apples to the pan and cook, stirring continuously, for 2–3 minutes, until they are just softened.

3 Add the cabbage, red wine vinegar, sugar, cloves, mustard seeds, raisins or currants, red wine or water and salt and pepper, stirring until well mixed. Bring to a boil over medium-high heat, stirring occasionally.

4 Cover and cook over medium-low heat for 35–40 minutes, until the cabbage is tender and the liquid is just absorbed, stirring occasionally. Add a little more red wine or water if the pan boils dry before the cabbage is tender. Just before serving, stir in the red currant jelly, if using, to sweeten and glaze the cabbage.

COOK'S TIPS

• If you find the cabbage difficult to cut up, use a long or double knife so that you can lean on both ends, and cut it on an old dish towel to stop it slipping.
• The whole dish could be cooked in, and served from, an electric frying pan.

NUTRITION NOTES

Per portion:

Calories	101
Fat, total	3.1g
saturated fat	0.2g
Protein	1.8g
Carbohydrate	17.6g
sugar, total	16.7g
Fiber—NSP	3.8g
Sodium	15.6mg

Broccoli and Cauliflower with Cider

The sauce in this dish is a good way of enhancing lightly steamed vegetables. It can be served with rice as a simple vegetarian meal.

INGREDIENTS

Serves 4

2 tablespoons olive oil
1 large onion, chopped or
    2 tablespoons dried onion
2 large carrots, chopped
1 large clove garlic or
    ½ teaspoon garlic purée
1 tablespoon dill seed
4 large sprigs apple mint
2 tablespoons all-purpose flour or, if
    you are on a wheat-free diet, use
    potato starch or cornstarch
1¼ cups cider
2 tablespoons soy sauce or, if you are on
    a wheat-free diet, wheat-free tamari
2 teaspoons mint jelly
1 pound broccoli florets
1 pound cauliflower florets

1 Heat the olive oil in a large saucepan or frying pan. Add the onion, carrots, garlic, dill seed and apple mint leaves and sauté over medium heat until the vegetables are almost cooked.

2 Meanwhile, steam the broccoli and cauliflower florets for 10 minutes or until just tender, then transfer to a large serving bowl. Keep the broccoli and cauliflower florets warm while you finish making the sauce.

3 Stir the flour into the sautéed vegetables. Then pour in the cider and simmer until the sauce looks glossy.

4 Pour the sautéed vegetables into a food processor. Add the soy sauce or tamari and the mint jelly and blend until finely puréed. If desired, return the sauce to the pan and heat through gently. Pour the warm sauce on the broccoli and cauliflower florets and serve immediately.

COOK'S TIPS

• If you would have difficulty chopping the vegetables for the sauce, you can cook them whole instead. They will be much easier to chop once they are cooked.

• Tamari is a type of soy sauce that does not contain wheat.

• You may find it easier to blend the vegetables for the sauce in the saucepan, using a hand-held blender.

• Try adding sunflower or pumpkin seeds to this dish. They contain GLAs which have been shown to reduce inflammation.

NUTRITION NOTES

Per portion:

Calories	182
Fat, total	7.7g
saturated fat	1.3g
Protein	9.9g
Carbohydrate	13.8g
sugar, total	11.4g
Fiber—NSP	6.5g
Sodium	38.1mg

Marinated Herrings

Herrings are oily fish, full of the nutrients that may reduce inflammation.

INGREDIENTS

Serves 4

4 herrings
⅔ cup white wine vinegar
2 teaspoons salt
12 black peppercorns
2 bay leaves
4 whole cloves
2 small onions, sliced or
    1 heaping teaspoon dried onion
bay leaves, to garnish

For the dressing
1 teaspoon coarse-grain mustard
3 tablespoons olive oil
1 tablespoon white wine vinegar
salt and ground black pepper

1 Preheat the oven to 325°F. Clean and bone the fish, if necessary, and use a sharp knife to divide each fish into two fillets.

2 Roll up the fillets tightly and place them packed together in an ovenproof dish so that they can't unroll.

4 Add the salt, spices and onions and bake for 1 hour. Let the herring cool in the liquid. Meanwhile, make the dressing. Whisk all the ingredients with a fork in a small bowl, or place in a screw-top jar and shake until combined. Garnish the fish with bay leaves and serve with the dressing.

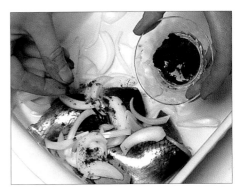

NUTRITION NOTES	
Per portion:	
Calories	420
Fat, total	31.4g
saturated fat	6.9g
Protein	31.6g
Carbohydrate	2.9g
sugar, total	2.1g
Fiber—NSP	0.5g
Sodium	211mg

3 Pour the vinegar on top and add water to just cover the fish.

--- COOK'S TIPS ---

• Buy the herring ready-boned and cleaned to make this dish easier to prepare.
• The fish do not need to be rolled up but can be layered in a pan to cook if you find them difficult to handle.

FISH AND MEAT DISHES

Oily fish, such as salmon, mackerel and sardines, contain beneficial

nutrients that can reduce inflammation in joints swollen by arthritis,

and you will find many recipes using oily fish in this section.

Or, try a low-fat meat dish, such as Chicken with Snow Peas and

Ginger and Glazed Sweet Potatoes with Bacon. All of the recipes

can be adapted easily to avoid the common arthritis trigger foods for

those who are following a special diet.

Salmon Steaks with Sorrel

Salmon and fresh sorrel are traditionally paired in French cooking—the sharp flavor of the sorrel balances the richness of the fish. If sorrel is not available use chopped watercress instead.

INGREDIENTS

Serves 2

2 salmon steaks (about 9 ounces each)
2 tablespoons olive oil
2 shallots, finely chopped or
    1 tablespoon dried onion
3 tablespoons whipping cream or, if you
    are on a dairy-free diet, soy cream
3½ ounces fresh sorrel leaves, washed
    and patted dry
salt and ground black pepper
fresh sage, to garnish

1 Season the salmon steaks with salt and freshly ground black pepper to taste. In a large saucepan, heat half of the olive oil over medium heat. Add the shallots or dried onion and sauté for 3–4 minutes, stirring frequently, until just softened.

NUTRITION NOTES

Per portion:

Calories	646
Fat, total	47.7g
saturated fat	11.9g
Protein	52.4g
Carbohydrate	1.8g
sugar, total	1.8g
Fiber—NSP	1.1g
Sodium	185mg

2 Add the cream and sorrel and cook for 3–4 minutes, until the sorrel is completely wilted, stirring constantly.

3 Meanwhile, brush a nonstick frying pan with the remaining oil. Place over medium heat until the olive oil is hot.

4 Add the salmon steaks to the frying pan and cook for about 5 minutes, turning once, until the flesh is opaque next to the bone. If you're not sure, pierce the salmon steaks with the tip of a sharp knife; if the fish are done the juices will run clear.

5 Arrange the salmon steaks on two warmed plates, garnish with sage and serve with the sorrel sauce.

COOK'S TIP

If your hands are weak you may find it easier to cook the salmon steaks in a microwave oven for 4–5 minutes, tightly covered, or according to the manufacturer's guidelines.

Grilled Mackerel with Spicy Dhal

Oily fish such as mackerel and sardines are often complemented by a tart accompaniment. In this recipe they are served with tamarind-flavored lentils.

INGREDIENTS

Serves 4

1 cup red lentils, or yellow split peas (soaked overnight)
4 cups water
2 tablespoons sunflower oil
½ teaspoon each mustard seeds, fennel seeds, cumin seeds and fenugreek seeds
1 teaspoon ground turmeric
3–4 dried red chiles, crumbled, or omit if you are on a solanacae-free diet
2 tablespoons tamarind paste
1 teaspoon brown sugar
2 tablespoons chopped cilantro
4 mackerel or 8 fresh sardines, cleaned
salt and ground black pepper
fresh red chile slices (optional) and finely chopped cilantro, to garnish
chapatis, to serve (optional)

1 Rinse the lentils or split peas, drain and put them in a saucepan. Add the water and bring to a boil. Lower the heat, partially cover the pan and simmer for 30–40 minutes, stirring occasionally, until the pulses are tender.

2 Heat the oil and add the mustard seeds. Cover and cook for a few seconds, until they pop. Add the other seeds, with the turmeric and chiles, if using, and fry for a few more seconds.

3 Stir in the pulses and season. Mix well; stir in the tamarind paste and sugar. Bring to a boil, then simmer for 10 minutes. Stir in the cilantro.

COOK'S TIP

If you have problems lifting heavy pans, remove the pulses from their cooking water using a slotted spoon. Empty the pan when the water is cold, which is much safer.

NUTRITION NOTES

Per portion:

Calories	688
Fat, total	38.1g
saturated fat	7.3g
Protein	53.0g
Carbohydrate	35.1g
sugar, total	1.5g
Fiber—NSP	3.0g
Sodium	138.5mg

---

4 Meanwhile, prepare the grill until very hot. Using a sharp knife, make six diagonal slashes on either side of each fish. Season inside and out.

5 Grill the fish for 5–7 minutes on each side, until the skin is blistered and crisp. Place each fish on a plate with the dhal and garnish with cilantro and chiles, if using. If desired, serve with chapatis, wheat-free if necessary.

Trout and Prosciutto Risotto Rolls

This is an imaginative dinner party dish that is bound to impress.

INGREDIENTS

Serves 4
4 trout fillets, skinned
prosciutto, 4 slices
caper berries, to garnish

For the risotto
2 tablespoons olive oil
8 large shrimp, peeled and deveined
1 onion, chopped
generous 1 cup risotto rice
7 tablespoons white wine
3 cups simmering fish or chicken stock
2 tablespoons dried porcini or
  chanterelle mushrooms, soaked for
  10 minutes in warm water to cover
salt and ground black pepper

1 Heat the oil in a deep frying pan or electric frying pan and fry the shrimp very briefly until flecked with pink. Lift out on a slotted spoon and transfer to a plate.

2 Add the chopped onion to the oil remaining in the pan and cook over low heat for 3–4 minutes, until soft.

3 Add the rice to the pan and stir for 3–4 minutes, until the grains are evenly coated in oil. Add 5 tablespoons of the wine and then the stock, a little at a time, stirring over low heat and letting the rice absorb the liquid before adding more.

4 Drain the mushrooms, reserving the liquid, and cut the larger ones in half. Toward the end of cooking, stir the mushrooms into the risotto with 1 tablespoon of the reserved mushroom liquid. Season to taste with salt and pepper.

5 Remove the pan from heat and stir in the shrimp. Preheat the oven to 375°F.

6 Take each trout fillet in turn, place a spoonful of risotto at one end and roll up. Wrap in a slice of prosciutto and place in a greased ovenproof dish.

7 Spoon any remaining risotto around the fish fillets and sprinkle on the rest of the wine. Cover loosely with aluminum foil and bake for 15–20 minutes, until the fish is tender. Spoon the risotto onto a platter, top with the trout rolls and garnish with capers. Unless you are on a wheat-free diet, whole-wheat bread goes well with this.

COOK'S TIP

If you find it too difficult to roll the fish, layer it with the prosciutto and risotto in the dish, sprinkle on the wine, cover tightly and bake for 15 minutes. Decorate with the capers and serve.

NUTRITION NOTES

Per portion:

Calories	513
Fat, total	15.8g
saturated fat	6.3g
Protein	41.5g
Carbohydrate	45.8g
sugar, total	2.3g
Fiber—NSP	7.3g
Sodium	842mg

Tuscan Tuna and Beans

A classic Italian mixture—tasty, filling and healthy. It's quick to make if you're short on time.

INGREDIENTS

Serves 4

1 red onion, or 6 scallions, trimmed
2 tablespoons smooth French mustard
1¼ cups olive oil
¼ cup white wine vinegar
2 tablespoons chopped fresh parsley
2 tablespoons chopped fresh chives
2 tablespoons chopped fresh tarragon or chervil
14-ounce can navy beans
14-ounce can kidney beans
8oz canned tuna in oil, drained and lightly flaked
parsley and chives, to garnish

1 Finely chop the red onion, or the scallions.

COOK'S TIP

If you have problems with your hands, it is much easier to chop herbs with scissors than with a knife.

2 In a small bowl, beat together the mustard, oil, vinegar, parsley, chives and tarragon or chervil. Drain the canned navy beans and kidney beans.

3 Combine the red onion or scallions, beans, flaked tuna and dressing in a large bowl. Toss well and serve, garnished with the extra parsley and whole chives.

--- NUTRITION NOTES ---

Per portion:

Calories	774
Fat, total	56.8g
saturated fat	8.2g
Protein	29.7g
Carbohydrate	38.6g
sugar, total	7.0g
Fiber—NSP	12.8g
Sodium	790mg

Stuffed Sardines

This Middle Eastern-inspired dish doesn't take a lot of preparation and is a meal in itself. Just serve with crisp green salad tossed in a fresh vinaigrette to make it complete.

INGREDIENTS

Serves 4

2 tablespoons olive oil
¾ cup whole-wheat bread crumbs or, if you are on a wheat-free diet, 2 small packages of plain potato chips, crushed
¼ cup golden raisins
½ cup pine nuts
1 onion, finely chopped or 1 tablespoon dried onion
2 ounces canned anchovy fillets, drained
¼ cup chopped fresh parsley
2 pounds fresh sardines, cleaned
salt and ground black pepper

2 Add the golden raisins, pine nuts, onion, anchovies, parsley and seasoning to the frying pan and mix well. If you are using chips, instead of bread crumbs, mix all of the stuffing ingredients in a bowl.

--- COOK'S TIP ---

If you find stuffing sardines difficult, simply lay the fish in the baking dish and spread the stuffing on top.

3 Stuff each sardine with the mixture. Close the fish firmly and place them in a shallow ovenproof dish, closely packed together.

4 Sprinkle the remaining stuffing mixture on the sardines and bake for 30 minutes. Try serving this on a bed of salad leaves, and pass lemon wedges, unless you are on a citrus-free diet, in which case you could drizzle cider vinegar on the dish.

1 Preheat the oven to 400°F. Heat the olive oil in a large frying pan and fry the bread crumbs until crisp and golden.

--- NUTRITION NOTES ---

Per portion:

Calories	655
Fat, total	37.7g
saturated fat	7.4g
Protein	54.2g
Carbohydrate	26.6g
sugar, total	11.7g
Fiber—NSP	1.4g
Sodium	907mg

Rice Cakes with Smoked Salmon

Smoked salmon goes perfectly with these elegant rice cakes. Salmon is an oily fish, containing beneficial nutrients that work to reduce inflammation.

INGREDIENTS

Serves 4

2 tablespoons dried porcini mushrooms
2 tablespoons olive oil
1 onion, chopped or
    1 tablespoon dried onion
generous 1 cup risotto rice
about 6 tablespoons white wine
about 3 cups fish or chicken stock
1 tablespoon chopped fresh parsley
1 tablespoon snipped fresh chives
1 teaspoon chopped fresh dill
1 egg, lightly beaten
about 3 tablespoons ground rice, plus
    extra for dusting
oil, for frying
6 ounces smoked salmon, chopped
baby asparagus spears, roasted, to serve
salt and ground black pepper
¼ cup sour cream or, if you are on a
    dairy-free diet, soy cream or
    coconut milk, to serve
radicchio and oak leaf salad, tossed in
    French dressing, to serve

NUTRITION NOTES

Per portion:

Calories	390
Fat, total	12.9g
saturated fat	3.4g
Protein	18.5g
Carbohydrate	45.7g
sugar, total	2.8g
Fiber—NSP	0.5g
Sodium	852mg

VARIATION

If you have any risotto left from another recipe, use it to make the rice cakes.

1 Place the porcini mushrooms in a bowl and cover with boiling water. Let soak for 15 minutes.

2 Heat the olive oil in a frying pan or saucepan and sauté the onion for 3–4 minutes, until soft.

3 Add the rice to the pan and cook, stirring, for 3–4 minutes, until the grains are thoroughly coated in oil. Pour in the wine and stock, a little at a time, stirring constantly over low heat. Check that the liquid has been absorbed before adding more.

COOK'S TIPS

• If you would find it difficult to make the patties, omit the egg and the ground rice and cook the risotto for slightly longer. Top with spoonfuls of sour cream, soy cream or coconut cream and sprinkle the chopped smoked salmon on top.
• Smoked salmon scraps, available at most supermarkets, will be fine for this dish and are much cheaper.

4 Drain the porcini mushrooms and chop them into small pieces. When the rice is tender, and all the liquid has been absorbed, stir in the mushrooms.

5 Add the parsley, chives, dill and seasoning to the risotto. Remove from heat and set aside for a few minutes to cool. Add the beaten egg and mix well. Then stir in enough ground rice to bind the mixture—it should be soft but manageable.

6 Dust your hands with ground rice and shape the mixture into four patties, about 5 inches in diameter and about ¾ inch thick.

7 Heat the oil in a frying pan and fry the rice cakes, in batches if necessary, for 4–5 minutes, until evenly browned on both sides. Drain on paper towels and cool slightly.

8 Place each rice cake on a plate and sprinkle on the chopped smoked salmon and asparagus spears. Serve with 1 tablespoon sour cream, soy cream or coconut milk and a fresh salad.

Sicilian Spaghetti with Sardines

This traditional dish is a great way to eat sardines, which are an excellent fish for building up your stock of anti-inflammatory alpha linolenic acid (ALA).

INGREDIENTS

Serves 4

12 fresh sardines, cleaned and boned
1 cup olive oil
1 onion or 1 tablespoon dried onion
¼ cup fresh dill, chopped
½ cup pine nuts
2 tablespoons raisins, soaked in water
½ cup fresh bread crumbs or,
  if you are on a wheat-free diet,
  crushed plain potato chips
1 pound spaghetti (wheat-free if you
  are on a wheat-free diet)
flour or, if you are on a wheat-free diet,
  potato starch or cornstarch, for dusting
salt and ground black pepper

1 Wash the sardines and pat dry on paper towels. Open them out flat, then cut in half lengthwise.

--- COOK'S TIP ---

If you have problems lifting heavy pans, place the spaghetti in a wire basket and cook in boiling water. You can lift out the spaghetti easily, and drain the water later, when cool.

2 Heat 2 tablespoons of the oil in a pan. Chop the onion and sauté until golden. Add the dill and cook gently for a minute or two. Add the pine nuts and raisins and season with salt and freshly ground black pepper to taste.

3 Meanwhile, place the bread crumbs in a frying pan and dry-fry until they are golden. Set aside.

4 Boil a large saucepan of salted water and add the spaghetti. Cook according to the instructions on the package, until the spaghetti is *al dente*.

5 Heat the remaining oil in a pan. Dust the sardines with flour and fry in the hot oil for 2–3 minutes. Drain on paper towels.

6 Drain the spaghetti. Add the onion mixture and toss well. Transfer the spaghetti mixture to a serving platter and arrange the fried sardines on top. Sprinkle with the toasted bread crumbs or chips and serve immediately.

--- NUTRITION NOTES ---

Per portion:

Calories	1,029
Fat, total	62g
saturated fat	9.2g
Protein	31.3g
Carbohydrate	91.2g
sugar, total	10.6g
Fiber—NSP	4.2g
Sodium	98mg

Grilled Salmon with Red Onion Marmalade

The sweet, caramelized red onions provide a perfect contrast to the fish, in color as well as flavor.

INGREDIENTS

Serves 4
4 salmon steaks, cut 1 inch thick
2 tablespoons olive oil
salt and ground black pepper
fresh flat-leaf parsley, to garnish

For the red onion marmalade
5 red onions, peeled
¼ cup olive oil
¾ cup red wine vinegar
¼ cup crème de cassis
¼ cup grenadine
¼ cup red wine

1 Brush the salmon steaks with the olive oil on both sides. Season the fish well with salt and ground black pepper.

2 Finely slice the onions or chop them if that is easier. Heat the oil in a saucepan and add the onions. Sauté for 5 minutes.

3 Stir in the remaining ingredients. Cook for about 10 minutes or until the onions are glazed. Season well.

4 Brush the fish with a little more oil, and cook on the grill for 4 minutes on each side. Transfer to warmed plates and garnish with parsley. Serve with the red onion marmalade.

NUTRITION NOTES

Per portion:

Calories	444
Fat, total	30.2g
saturated fat	4.7g
Protein	25.3g
Carbohydrate	8.17g
sugar, total	8.17g
Fiber—NSP	0.0g
Sodium	57.1mg

COOK'S TIPS

• If you cannot find crème de cassis and grenadine, replace both of these ingredients with red wine.

• Fish cooks well on the grill, but make sure it is at least 1 inch thick to make it easy to turn when cooking.

Salmon Risotto with Cucumber and Tarragon

An easy but tasty dish that can be served from the pot it was cooked in. Salmon is an oily fish, rich in ALA (alpha linolenic acid). This is beneficial to arthritis sufferers, as it can help to reduce inflammation and joint pain.

INGREDIENTS

Serves 4

2 tablespoons olive oil
small bunch of scallions, white parts only, chopped with scissors
½ cucumber, peeled, seeded and chopped (see Cook's Tip)
1¼ cups risotto rice
5 cups hot chicken or fish stock
⅔ cup dry white wine
1 pound salmon fillet, skinned and diced
3 tablespoons chopped fresh tarragon
salt and ground black pepper

1 Heat the oil in a large saucepan or electric frying pan and add the scallions and the cucumber. Cook for 2–3 minutes without letting the scallions color.

--- COOK'S TIP ---

If you would find peeling and seeding the cucumber difficult, just chop it with skin and seeds intact.

2 Stir in the rice, then add the stock and wine. bring to a boil, then lower the heat and simmer, uncovered, for 10 minutes, stirring occasionally.

3 Stir in the diced salmon and season to taste with salt and ground black pepper. Continue cooking for another 5 minutes, stirring occasionally, then switch off the heat. Cover and let stand for 5 minutes.

4 Remove the lid, add the chopped fresh tarragon and mix lightly to combine. Serve the risotto immediately, in warmed bowls.

--- NUTRITION NOTES ---

Per portion:

Calories	606
Fat, total	19.5g
saturated fat	2.9g
Protein	32.4g
Carbohydrate	66.9g
sugar, total	0.7g
Fiber—NSP	0.2g
Sodium	596mg

Roast Lamb with Spiced Apricot Stuffing

Cinnamon, cumin and apricots are complementary partners in a bulghur wheat stuffing used in this easy-to-carve roast.

INGREDIENTS

Serves 6

½ cup bulghur wheat or, if you are on a wheat-free diet, brown rice (see Cook's Tips)
2 tablespoons olive oil
1 small onion, finely chopped or 1½ teaspoons dried onion
1 garlic clove, crushed or 1 teaspoon garlic purée
1 teaspoon ground cinnamon
1 teaspoon cumin
¾ cup chopped dried apricots
⅔ cup pine nuts
1 boned shoulder of lamb, about 4–4½ pounds
½ cup red wine
½ cup lamb stock
salt and ground black pepper
fresh mint sprigs, to garnish

1 Place the bulghur wheat in a bowl and add enough warm water to cover. Let soak for 1 hour, then drain thoroughly.

2 Heat the oil in a saucepan. Add the onion and garlic and cook for about 5 minutes. Stir in the bulghur wheat, cinnamon, cumin, apricots and pine nuts and season to taste. Let cool.

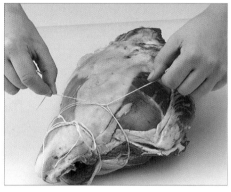

3 Preheat the oven to 350°F. Open out the shoulder of lamb and spread on the stuffing. Roll it up firmly and tie tightly with string. Place in a roasting pan. Roast for 1 hour, then pour the red wine and stock into the roasting pan.

4 Roast the lamb for 30 more minutes, then transfer to a heated plate, cover with foil and let the meat rest for 15–20 minutes before carving.

5 Meanwhile, skim the surface fat from the wine-flavored stock in the roasting pan. Place the pan over high heat and let the gravy bubble for a few minutes, stirring occasionally to incorporate any sediment. Carve the lamb neatly, arrange the slices on a serving platter and pour on the gravy. Serve immediately, garnished with mint.

NUTRITION NOTES

Per portion:

Calories	749
Fat, total	52.5g
saturated fat	20.8g
Protein	44.8g
Carbohydrate	22.1g
sugar, total	11.7g
Fiber—NSP	2.3g
Sodium	272mg

COOK'S TIPS

• If you are using brown rice, add it to the cooked onion and garlic at Step 2 with about 1¼ cups stock. Bring to a boil and simmer until the rice is cooked. Then add the spices, apricots and pine nuts.
• If you would have problems stuffing and tying the lamb, leave it whole and roast for 40 minutes per pound, plus 20 minutes extra. Add the stock and wine halfway through, and cook the stuffing separately in a casserole.

Chicken with Snow Peas and Ginger

INGREDIENTS

Serves 4

4 boned and skinned chicken breasts
8 ounces snow peas
3 tablespoons olive oil
3 garlic cloves, finely chopped or
    2 teaspoons garlic purée
1-inch piece fresh ginger root,
    freshly grated or 2 teaspoons
    powdered ginger
5–6 scallions, cut into 1½-inch lengths
    with scissors
2 teaspoons sesame oil
boiled rice, to serve; parsley, to garnish

For the marinade
1 teaspoon cornstarch
1 tablespoon light soy sauce, wheat-free
    if you are on a wheat-free diet
1 tablespoon medium dry sherry
1 tablespoon vegetable oil

For the sauce
1 teaspoon cornstarch
2–3 teaspoons dark soy sauce, wheat-
    free if you are on a wheat-free diet
½ cup chicken stock
2 tablespoons oyster sauce, or omit if
    you are on a wheat-free diet

1 Cut the chicken into thick strips. For the marinade, blend together the cornstarch and soy sauce. Stir in the sherry and oil. Pour onto the chicken, toss lightly, and let sit for 30 minutes.

2 Trim the snow peas and plunge into a pan of boiling salted water. Bring back to a boil and then drain and refresh under cold running water.

COOK'S TIP

If you have trouble with your hands, put the snow peas in a sieve. Fill a pan with water, bring to a boil, then lower in the sieve with the snow peas for 1 minute. Remove and refresh under cold running water.

3 To make the sauce, combine the cornstarch, soy sauce, stock and oyster sauce and set aside.

4 Heat 1 tablespoon of the olive oil in a wok and add the garlic, ginger and scallions. Stir-fry for 30 seconds. Add the chicken with its marinade, and cook briskly for a couple of minutes. Lower the heat, cover the wok and simmer for 15 minutes or until the chicken pieces are cooked through. Stir in the sesame oil, the sauce and the snow peas. Cook for another couple of minutes. Serve with boiled rice and garnish with parsley.

NUTRITION NOTES

Per portion:

Calories	290
Fat, total	13.7g
saturated fat	2.0g
Protein	38.9g
Carbohydrate	3.1g
sugar, total	2.3g
Fiber—NSP	1.6g
Sodium	306mg

Chicken with Beans

This substantial casserole is bursting with flavor, texture and color.

INGREDIENTS

Serves 4

10 ounces dried kidney or other beans, soaked overnight, then cooked in fast boiling water for 20 minutes, or 14-ounce can kidney beans, drained
8 chicken portions, such as thighs and drumsticks
12 strips bacon
2 large onions, thinly sliced or 2 tablespoons dried onion
1 cup dry white wine
½ teaspoon chopped fresh sage or oregano, or ¼ teaspoon dried
½ teaspoon chopped fresh rosemary, or ¼ teaspoon dried
generous pinch of grated nutmeg
⅔ cup sour cream or, if you are on a dairy-free diet, plain soy yogurt
1 tablespoon chili powder or, if you are on a solanacae-free diet, ground ginger
salt and ground black pepper
sprigs of rosemary, to garnish
lemon wedges, to serve (optional)

1 Rinse and drain the beans well and trim the chicken pieces. Season the chicken with salt and pepper.

2 Arrange the bacon around the sides and on the bottom of an ovenproof dish. Sprinkle on half the sliced onion and then half the kidney beans, followed by another layer of onion and then the remaining beans.

3 Preheat the oven to 350°F. Pour the wine into a large bowl and add the sage or oregano, rosemary and nutmeg. Combine the wine and the herbs and then pour onto the onion and beans in the casserole dish.

4 In another bowl, combine the sour cream or soy yogurt and the chili powder or ground ginger.

5 Toss the chicken in the sour cream mixture, and place on top of the beans.

6 Cover with aluminum foil and bake for 1¼–1½ hours, removing the foil for the last 15 minutes of cooking. Garnish with sprigs of rosemary and serve with the lemon wedges, if using.

—————— COOK'S TIP ——————

Kidney beans are very nutritious, but it is important to cook the dried ones in fast boiling water for 20 minutes, in order to kill the toxins they contain.

—————— NUTRITION NOTES ——————

Per portion:

Calories	665
Fat, total	31.9g
saturated fat	12.2g
Protein	57.5g
Carbohydrate	29.0g
sugar, total	12.1g
Fiber—NSP	7.8g
Sodium	1,531mg

Stuffed Fennel

Fennel not only tastes delicious, but it divides into neat boat shapes, ideal for stuffing.

INGREDIENTS

Serves 4
2 large bulbs fennel
3 eggs
2 tablespoons olive oil
1 onion, chopped or
   1 tablespoon dried onion
2 chicken breasts, skinned and boned
2½ cups trimmed and chopped
   oyster mushrooms
¼ cup all-purpose flour or, if you are on a
   wheat-free diet, potato starch or cornstarch
1¼ cups homemade or canned chicken
   broth, boiling
1 teaspoon Dijon mustard
2 tablespoons sherry
salt and ground black pepper
fresh parsley sprigs, to garnish
boiled rice, to serve

1 Preheat the oven to 375°F. Cut off the base of the fennel and pull each bulb apart into four pieces (save the central part). Boil the fennel in salted water for 3–4 minutes, then drain and let to cool. Boil the eggs for 10 minutes. Let cool, then peel and set aside.

2 Finely chop the central part of the fennel. Sauté gently in oil with the onion for 3–4 minutes.

3 Cut the chicken into pieces and add to the frying pan with the mushrooms. Cook over medium heat for 6 minutes, stirring frequently. Add the flour, potato or cornstarch and remove from heat.

4 Gradually add the chicken broth, making sure the thickener is completely absorbed. Return to the heat and simmer until thickened, stirring constantly. Chop one of the eggs into the chicken mixture and add the mustard, sherry and seasoning to taste.

5 Arrange the fennel in a baking dish. Spoon the filling into each one, cover with foil and bake for 20–25 minutes. Serve on a bed of rice, garnished with the remaining eggs, quartered, and parsley.

NUTRITION NOTES

Per portion:

Calories	91
Fat, total	6.0g
saturated fat	0.8g
Protein	2. 8g
Carbohydrate	4.8g
sugar, total	3.6g
Fiber—NSP	2.9g
Sodium	193mg

COOK'S TIP

If you find the fennel difficult to cut, cook it before trying to cut it. It will be much easier to deal with once it is cooked.

Glazed Sweet Potatoes with Bacon

Bacon is the perfect addition to these melt-in-your-mouth sugar-topped potatoes. This is a good basic dish if you are on a solanacae-free diet.

INGREDIENTS

Serves 4

oil, for greasing
2 pounds sweet potatoes
½ cup light brown sugar
2 tablespoons lemon juice or, if you are on a citrus-free diet,
    2 tablespoons cider vinegar
3 tablespoons olive oil
4 strips bacon, cut into matchsticks
salt and ground black pepper
chopped flat-leaf parsley, to garnish

1 Preheat the oven to 375°F and lightly oil a shallow ovenproof dish. Cut each unpeeled sweet potato crosswise into three pieces and steam for about 25 minutes, until they are just tender. Let the sweet potatoes cool.

2 When the potatoes are cool enough to handle, peel and slice thickly.

3 Arrange the potatoes in a single layer, overlapping the slices, in the prepared dish. Sprinkle the sugar on top of the sweet potatoes.

NUTRITION NOTES	
Per portion:	
Calories	378
Fat, total	7.5g
saturated fat	2.1g
Protein	6.8g
Carbohydrate	77.0g
sugar, total	41.9g
Fiber—NSP	5.4g
Sodium	483mg

------ COOK'S TIP ------

If you find it too difficult to use a knife to cut the bacon into matchsticks, try using scissors instead.

4 Lightly sprinkle on the lemon juice or cider vinegar and drizzle with oil. Top the sweet potatoes with the bacon and season with salt and freshly ground black pepper to taste. Bake uncovered for 35–40 minutes, basting once or twice.

5 Preheat the broiler to high. Sprinkle the potatoes with parsley. Place under the broiler for 2–3 minutes until the potatoes are browned and the bacon is crispy. Serve hot.

VEGETARIAN DISHES

This delicious selection of recipes includes dishes that use familiar

vegetables, such as the zucchini and carrots in Three Color Tagliatelle,

and others that encourage you to experiment with different ingredients.

Try Swiss chard leaves in a traditional French omelet, or make the

tasty Jerusalem Artichoke Risotto.

The recipes in this section are nutritious, fairly easy to prepare and

follow the guidelines for a low-fat meat-free diet.

Three Color Tagliatelle

This attractive dish might look difficult to prepare, but the colorful vegetable "ribbons" are much easier to cut than you would think.

INGREDIENTS

Serves 4

2 large zucchini
2 large carrots
9 ounces fresh tagliatelle, wheat-free if you are on a wheat-free diet
¼ cup extra virgin olive oil
flesh of 2 roasted garlic cloves, plus extra roasted garlic cloves, to serve (optional), or 2 teaspoons crushed raw garlic or garlic purée
salt and ground black pepper
2 tablespoons toasted sunflower seeds, to serve (optional)

1 Using a vegetable peeler, cut the zucchini and carrots into long thin ribbons.

2 Bring a large pan of salted water to a boil. Put the carrots and zucchini ribbons into a sieve. Sink them into a boiling water. Bring the water back to a boil and boil for 30 seconds, then remove and set aside.

3 Cook the pasta according to the instructions on the package, until it is *al dente*. You may prefer to cook it in a wire basket. That way, you can lift out the food easily, and empty the heavy pan of water when it is cool.

4 Drain the pasta and return it to the pan. Add the vegetable ribbons, oil, garlic and seasoning and toss over medium to high heat until the pasta and vegetables are glistening with oil. Serve immediately, with extra roasted garlic and sunflower seeds, if desired.

--- COOK'S TIPS ---

• To roast garlic, put a whole head of garlic on a lightly oiled baking sheet. Place in an oven preheated to 350°F and roast for about 30 minutes. Remove the garlic from the oven and set aside. When cool enough to handle, dig out the flesh from the cloves with a small, sharp spoon.
• If you are struggling with the vegetable peeler, use more zucchini, which are easier to prepare, and fewer carrots.

--- NUTRITION NOTES ---

Per portion:

Calories	240
Fat, total	15.4g
saturated fat	2.09g
Protein	5.05g
Carbohydrate	21.7g
sugar, total	6.4g
Fiber—NSP	2.3g
Sodium	49mg

Braised Chinese Vegetables

The original recipe calls for no less than 18 different ingredients to represent the 18 Buddhas, but nowadays four to six items are regarded as quite enough.

INGREDIENTS

Serves 4

¼ ounce dried black fungus (wood ears)
3 ounces straw mushrooms, drained
3 ounces sliced bamboo shoots, drained
2 ounces snow peas
4 ounces tofu
6 ounces Chinese cabbage
3–4 tablespoons vegetable oil
1 teaspoon salt
½ teaspoon light brown sugar
1 tablespoon light soy sauce, which should be wheat-free tamari if you are on a wheat-free diet
few drops sesame oil (optional)
2 tablespoons pumpkin seeds (optional)

1 Soak the black fungus (wood ears) in cold water for 20–25 minutes, then rinse and discard the hard stems, if any. Cut the straw mushrooms in half lengthwise, if large—keep them whole, if small. Rinse and drain the bamboo shoot slices. Trim the snow peas. Cut the tofu into about 12 small pieces. Cut the Chinese cabbage into small pieces about the same size as the snow peas.

2 Harden the tofu pieces by placing them in a wok or saucepan of boiling water for about 2 minutes. Remove with a slotted spoon and drain.

3 Heat the oil in the wok or saucepan and lightly brown the tofu pieces on both sides. Remove with a slotted spoon and keep warm.

4 Stir-fry all the vegetables in the wok or saucepan for about 1½ minutes, then add the tofu pieces, salt, sugar and soy sauce. Continue stirring for another minute, then cover and braise for 2–3 minutes. Sprinkle with sesame oil and pumpkin seeds, if using, and serve immediately.

COOK'S TIP

Remember that you can use scissors to cut up all the ingredients if you find it easier.

——— NUTRITION NOTES ———

Per portion:

Calories	126
Fat, total	10.6g
saturated fat	1.4g
Protein	5.6g
Carbohydrate	2.0g
sugar, total	1.6g
Fiber—NSP	1.3g
Sodium	274mg

Cilantro Omelet Parcels with Vegetables

These tasty egg rolls are packed with antioxidants such as vitamins C and E, while ginger is well known for its anti-inflammatory properties.

INGREDIENTS

Serves 4

4½ ounces broccoli, cut into
  small florets
2 tablespoons peanut oil
½-inch piece fresh ginger root, finely
  grated or 1 teaspoon ginger purée
  or 1 teaspoon powdered ginger
1 large garlic clove, crushed or
  1 teaspoon garlic purée
2 red chiles, seeded and finely sliced, or
  omit if you are on a solanacae-free diet
4 scallions, sliced diagonally
3 cups shredded bok choy
2 cups cilantro leaves,
  plus extra to garnish
½ cup bean sprouts
3 tablespoons black bean sauce, wheat-
  free if you are on a wheat-free diet
4 eggs
salt and freshly ground black pepper

1 Put the broccoli florets in the top of a steamer, submerge them in boiling water for 2 minutes, remove, then refresh under cold running water.

2 Meanwhile, heat 1 tablespoon of the oil in a frying pan or wok. Add the ginger, garlic and half the chile, if using, and stir-fry for 1 minute.

3 Add the scallions, broccoli and bok choy to the pan or wok, and stir-fry for about 2 more minutes, tossing the vegetables continuously to prevent sticking and to cook evenly. Roughly chop three-quarters of the cilantro and add.

4 Add the bean sprouts and stir-fry for 1 minute, then add the black bean sauce and heat through for 1 minute. Remove from heat. Keep warm.

5 Whisk the eggs and season well. Heat a little oil in a frying pan and add a quarter of the beaten egg. Swirl on the bottom of the pan, then add a quarter of the remaining cilantro leaves. Cook the omelet until set. Turn out and keep warm. Make three more omelets. Add more oil when necessary.

6 Spoon the stir-fry onto the omelets, roll up and cut in half. Garnish with cilantro leaves and chile.

─── NUTRITION NOTES ───	
Per portion:	
Calories	150
Fat, total	11.5g
saturated fat	2.7g
Protein	9.0g
Carbohydrate	2.7g
sugar, total	2.4g
Fiber—NSP	1.7g
Sodium	327mg

Teriyaki Soba Noodles with Asparagus

You can, of course, buy ready-made teriyaki sauce, but it is easy to prepare at home using ingredients that are now readily available at supermarkets and Asian stores. Japanese soba noodles are made from buckwheat flour, which gives them a unique texture and color, and makes them suitable for those on wheat-free diets!

INGREDIENTS

Serves 4

1 tablespoon sesame seeds
12 ounces soba noodles
2 tablespoons sesame oil
7 ounces asparagus tips
2 tablespoons peanut or vegetable oil
8 ounces block of tofu
2 scallions, cut diagonally
1 carrot, cut into matchsticks (optional)
½ teaspoon chile flakes or omit if on a
  solanacae-free diet
salt and ground black pepper

For the teriyaki sauce
¼ cup dark soy sauce, wheat-free if you
  are on a wheat-free diet
¼ cup Japanese sake or dry sherry
¼ cup mirin, wheat-free if you are on a
  wheat-free diet
1 teaspoon sugar

NUTRITION NOTES	
Per portion:	
Calories	492
Fat, total	16.8g
saturated fat	2.0g
Protein	13.4g
Carbohydrate	72.1g
sugar, total	6.1g
Fiber—NSP	4.3g
Sodium	871mg

1 Toast the sesame seeds in a dry frying pan over medium heat for 2 minutes, tossing frequently. Set aside.

2 Cook the noodles according to the instructions on the package, then drain and rinse under cold running water. Set aside.

3 Heat the sesame oil in a ridged broiler pan or in a baking sheet placed under the broiler until very hot. Turn down the heat to medium, then cook the asparagus for 8–10 minutes, turning frequently, until tender and browned. Set aside.

HEALTH BENEFITS
Sesame seeds are an excellent source of the antioxidant vitamin E, which acts as a natural preservative, preventing oxidation and strengthening the heart and nerves.

4 Meanwhile, heat the oil in a frying pan, wok or electric frying pan until very hot. Add the tofu and fry for 8–10 minutes, until golden, turning it occasionally to crisp all sides. Remove from the pan and let drain on paper towels. Cut into ½-inch slices.

5 To prepare the teriyaki sauce, combine all of the ingredients together, then pour into a frying pan, wok or electric frying pan and heat gently.

6 Toss in the noodles and stir. Heat through for 1–2 minutes, then spoon into warmed serving bowls with the tofu and asparagus. Sprinkle on the scallions, and the carrot and chile flakes, if using them. Season, then add the sesame seeds and serve.

Tofu and Vegetables

You might like to add sunflower seeds to this, as they contain the anti-inflammatory acid, GLA.

INGREDIENTS

Serves 4

2 8-ounce blocks smoked tofu, cubed
3 tablespoons soy sauce or, if you are on a wheat-free diet, wheat-free tamari
2 tablespoons dry sherry or vermouth
1 tablespoon sesame oil, plus extra to serve (optional)
3 tablespoons peanut or sunflower oil
2 leeks, thinly sliced
2 carrots, cut in sticks
1 large zucchini, thinly sliced
4 ounces baby corn, halved
4 ounces button or shiitake mushrooms, sliced
1 tablespoon sesame seeds
1 package of noodles, cooked, or, if you are on a wheat-free diet, rice noodles or wheat-free pasta

1 Marinate the tofu in the soy sauce, sherry or vermouth and sesame oil for at least half an hour. Drain and reserve the marinade.

—— VARIATION ——

Tofu is also excellent marinated and threaded onto small skewers, then lightly grilled. Serve the tofu with pita bread and a green salad.

2 Heat the peanut or sunflower oil in a wok and stir-fry the tofu cubes until they are browned all over. Remove and reserve.

3 Stir-fry the leeks, carrots, zucchini and baby corn, for about 2 minutes. Add the sliced mushrooms and cook for another minute.

4 Return the tofu to the wok and pour in the marinade. Heat until bubbling, then sprinkle on the sesame seeds. Serve as soon as possible with the hot cooked noodles or pasta, dressed in a little sesame oil, if desired.

—— NUTRITION NOTES ——

Per portion:

Calories	425
Fat, total	20.8g
saturated fat	4.0g
Protein	18.6g
Carbohydrate	41.2g
sugar, total	5.1g
Fiber—NSP	3.4g
Sodium	520mg

Lima Bean and Pesto Pasta

This rich and creamy pasta dish is simplicity itself to make, and yet it tastes sensational.

INGREDIENTS

Serves 4

8 ounces pasta shapes, wheat-free if you are on a wheat-free diet
fresh nutmeg, grated
2 tablespoons extra virgin olive oil
14-ounce can lima beans, drained
3 tablespoons pesto sauce but see Cook's Tip if you are on a dairy-free diet
⅔ cup light cream or, if you are on a dairy-free diet, soy milk
salt and ground black pepper

To serve

3 tablespoons pine nuts
cheese, grated (optional), omit if on a dairy-free diet
sprigs of fresh basil, to garnish (optional)

1 Boil the pasta in a large saucepan until it is *al dente*, then drain, leaving it a little wet. Return the pasta to the pan, season, and stir in the grated nutmeg and olive oil.

COOK'S TIP

Most pesto contains Parmesan cheese, which should be avoided if you are on a dairy-free diet. If you cannot find a ready-made pesto that is suitable for your diet, it is easy to make your own. Follow a recipe for making pesto, substituting a hard sheep's milk cheese such as Pecorino for the Parmesan.

2 Heat the beans in a saucepan with the pesto and cream, stirring the mixture until it begins to simmer. Toss the beans and pesto into the pasta and mix well.

3 Serve the pasta in bowls and top with pine nuts and a little grated cheese, if desired. Garnish with basil sprigs, if desired, and serve immediately.

NUTRITION NOTES

Per portion:

Calories	528
Fat, total	27.2g
saturated fat	7.4g
Protein	17.5g
Carbohydrate	56.8g
sugar, total	5.1g
Fiber—NSP	6.4g
Sodium	494mg

Mushroom and Sunflower Seed Flan

The flan can be prepared in advance and is good warm or cold. Spinach is an excellent source of antioxidants, which protect against cancer, as well as minimizing the joint damage caused by arthritis.

INGREDIENTS

Serves 4

1 cup whole-wheat flour or, if you are on a wheat-free diet, ½ cup chickpea flour plus ½ cup rice flour
3 ounces butter or dairy-free spread
3 tablespoons walnut or sunflower oil
5 ounces fresh baby corn
2 ounces sunflower seeds
7 ounces button mushrooms, wiped
3 ounces fresh spinach or defrosted frozen leaf spinach
juice 1 lemon or, if you are on a citrus-free diet, 2 tablespoons cider vinegar
salt and ground black pepper

1 Heat the oven to 350°F. Make the pastry by rubbing the butter or spread into the flour.

2 Add enough water to make a firm dough. Roll it out and line a 9–10-inch tart pan. You can press the pastry out into the flan dish rather than rolling it if you have problems with your hands. This may also be easier if you are using wheat-free flours, which make crumbly pastry.

3 Prick the bottom of the pastry shell, line it with aluminum foil, and weight it with beans or rice. Bake for 10 minutes with the foil, then 10 minutes without, so that the pastry becomes crisp.

4 Heat the oil in a pan and add the corn and sunflower seeds. Fry briskly until they are browned all over.

5 Add the mushrooms, reduce the heat slightly and cook for about 3 minutes. Add the chopped spinach, stir well, cover the pan and cook for another couple of minutes.

6 Add the lemon juice or vinegar and season well. Make sure the ingredients are well amalgamated, then spoon them into the pastry shell. Serve the flan immediately, or, if you prefer, let cool and serve at room temperature.

COOK'S TIP

If your hands are stiff and painful, combine the fat and flour in a food processor.

NUTRITION NOTES

Per portion:

Calories	447
Fat, total	32.0g
saturated fat	11.7g
Protein	12.5g
Carbohydrate	28.8g
sugar, total	2.5g
Fiber—NSP	4.6g
Sodium	401mg

Jerusalem Artichoke Risotto

The delicious and distinctive flavor of Jerusalem artichokes makes this simple and warming risotto something special.

INGREDIENTS

Serves 4

14 ounces Jerusalem artichokes
4 tablespoons olive oil
1 onion, finely chopped or
  1 tablespoon dried onion
1 garlic clove, crushed or
  1 teaspoon puréed garlic
1½ cups risotto rice
½ cup white wine
4 cups simmering vegetable stock
2 teaspoons chopped fresh thyme
½ cup freshly grated Parmesan cheese,
  plus extra to serve, or, if you are on a
  dairy-free diet, 1½ ounces chopped
  black olives
salt and ground black pepper
fresh thyme sprigs, to garnish

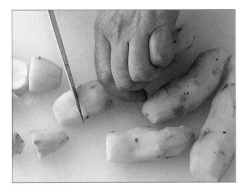

1 Peel the artichokes, cut them into pieces and steam over boiling water. Mash them with a potato masher or purée them in a bowl with a hand-held blender. Add 1 tablespoon olive oil and season with salt.

—— COOK'S TIP ——

If you find the artichokes difficult to peel, scrub them well and cook them without peeling. It will be much easier to peel them when they are cooked.

2 Heat the remaining oil in a pan and sauté the onion and garlic for 5–6 minutes, until soft. Add the rice and cook for about 2 minutes or until the grains are translucent around the edges.

3 Pour in the wine, stir until it has been absorbed, then add the stock, a ladleful at a time, letting it be absorbed before adding more. When you have one ladleful of stock left, stir in the artichokes and the thyme.

4 Continue cooking until the risotto is creamy and the artichokes are hot. Stir in the Parmesan or black olives and season to taste.

5 Remove the risotto from heat, cover the pan and let to stand for a few minutes. Serve garnished with thyme and sprinkled with Parmesan cheese, if using.

—— NUTRITION NOTES ——

Per portion:

Calories	483
Fat, total	16.7g
saturated fat	3.7g
Protein	13.2g
Carbohydrate	65.6g
sugar, total	3.8g
Fiber—NSP	4.2g
Sodium	701mg

Red Onion and Broccoli Risotto

INGREDIENTS

Serves 4

2 tablespoons olive oil
2 red onions, finely sliced or
    2 tablespoons dried onion
2 garlic cloves, finely sliced or
    1 teaspoon garlic purée
5 ounces risotto rice
1¼ cups dry white wine
2½ cups water
7 ounces broccoli florets, steamed for a
    few minutes, until partially cooked
9 ounces smoked or marinated
    tofu, cubed
7-ounce can water chestnuts, drained
    and halved
2 ounces roasted salted cashews
salt and ground black pepper

1 Heat the oil in a large pan. Gently
cook the onion and garlic until soft.

2 Add the rice, wine and water,
stirring gently. Bring to a simmer
and cook for 10–15 minutes or until
the rice is soft and the liquid has been
absorbed. Add more liquid if necessary.

3 Add the broccoli florets, tofu,
water chestnuts and cashews
to the rice. Mix well and season with
salt and pepper to taste. Serve the
risotto warm or cold.

—— NUTRITION NOTES ——

Per portion:

Calories	365
Fat, total	15.6g
saturated fat	2.4g
Protein	14.3g
Carbohydrate	41.4g
sugar, total	7.5g
Fiber—NSP	2.7g
Sodium	51.6mg

—— COOK'S TIP ——

For even creamier results, bring the wine
and water to a simmer in a separate pan,
and then add to the rice a ladleful at a
time, letting it be absorbed before adding
the next.

Roast Vegetables with Artichokes

A colorful medley of vegetables,
perfect for winter evenings.

INGREDIENTS

Serves 4

2 14-ounce cans artichoke hearts
2 14-ounce cans fava beans
¼ cup olive oil
4 turnips, peeled and sliced thickly, or
    scrubbed and left whole
4 medium carrots, scrubbed and
    left whole
4 leeks, sliced thickly
2 large zucchini, chopped into large
    chunks or 4 small zucchini wiped,
    trimmed, and left whole
3½ ounces fresh spinach or frozen
    spinach, defrosted
2 tablespoons pumpkin seeds
1 tablespoon ketchup
ground black pepper
rice or baked potatoes to serve (optional)

1 Preheat the oven to 350°F. Drain the
artichoke hearts and fava beans. Put
the oil in the bottom of a casserole or
deep baking pan, then add all the other
ingredients apart from the ketchup,
pumpkin seeds and black pepper.

2 Cover the casserole. Cook the
vegetables for 30–40 minutes or
until the turnips are soft.

3 Add the pumpkin seeds, ketchup
and pepper. Serve alone or with
rice, baked potatoes or bread.

—— COOK'S TIP ——

If you are in a hurry, cook the vegetables in
a microwave on high for 4 minutes, then
transfer to the oven for 20 minutes.

—— NUTRITION NOTES ——

Per portion:

Calories	373
Fat, total	13.7g
saturated fat	2.1g
Protein	24.1g
Carbohydrate	43.0g
sugar, total	15.7g
Fiber—NSP	16.3g
Sodium	657mg

Potato, Leek and Apple Casserole

Apples are the unusual ingredient used to flavor this dish. A perfect meal on a cold winter evening.

INGREDIENTS

Serves 6

3 pounds floury potatoes, or, if you are on a solanacae-free diet, sweet potatoes
3 leeks, sliced
4 tablespoons olive oil
3 onions, roughly chopped
small head of celery, chopped
2 large apples,
2 ounces potato flour or, if you are on a solanacae-free diet, cornstarch
scant 2 cups milk or, if you are on a dairy-free diet, soy milk
3 ounces pumpkin seeds, partially pulverized in a food processor
1 pound sesame seeds
salt and ground black pepper

1 Preheat the oven to 350°F. Scrub the potatoes or sweet potatoes well and cut into thin slices. Par-cook them, with the leeks, in a steamer or microwave for about 10 minutes or until softened.

2 Lightly grease a shallow, ovenproof dish. Arrange half of the potatoes and all of the leeks in a layer at the bottom of the dish.

3 Peel, core and dice the apples. Heat 3 tablespoons of the oil in a pan and gently cook the onions, celery and apple until the onion and celery are soft.

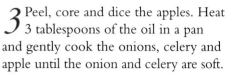

4 Add the potato flour or cornstarch, stir well, then gradually add the milk and continue to cook until the sauce thickens slightly. Spoon this mixture onto the potatoes and leeks, then cover with the remaining slices of potato.

5 Brush the top of the potatoes with the remaining 1 tablespoon oil. Season, then sprinkle on the pumpkin and sesame seeds.

6 Bake for 20–30 minutes or until the dish is heated through and the potatoes on top are lightly browned. Serve immediately.

--- COOK'S TIP ---

If you have trouble slicing the potatoes or sweet potatoes, cook them whole and slice them when cooked.

--- NUTRITION NOTES ---

Per portion:

Calories	446
Fat, total	15.1g
saturated fat	7.1g
Protein	12.4g
Carbohydrate	69.1g
sugar, total	16.2g
Fiber—NSP	6.6g
Sodium	69.7mg

Buckwheat Crêpes with Mushroom Sauce

These crêpes are very adaptable and can be used with sweet fillings as well as savory.

INGREDIENTS

Serves 4

1 cup buckwheat flour
1 large egg
½ cup water
⅔ cup milk or, if you are on a dairy-
    free diet, soy milk
2 tablespoons olive oil
2 medium leeks, wiped and sliced
1 clove garlic, finely chopped, or
    1 teaspoon puréed garlic
7 ounces button mushrooms, wiped
    and sliced
1 tablespoon potato flour or, if you are
    on a solanacae-free diet, cornstarch
scant 2 cups milk or,
    if you are on a dairy-free diet,
    unsweetened soy milk
2 tablespoons corn (canned or frozen
    will do fine)
2 ounces chopped toasted hazelnuts
salt and ground black pepper
chopped fresh parsley

1 To make the crêpes, mix the flour, egg, water, milk and a pinch of salt in a food processor, then let the mixture stand for 10–15 minutes.

2 Heat a crêpe pan with a tiny dribble of oil. Pour one small ladleful of the mixture into the pan and cook quickly on both sides. The crêpes should be quite thin, and you should get eight out of the batter. Reserve half of the pancakes to use later. Set them aside with a layer of plastic wrap or waxed paper between each one.

3 To make the filling for the crêpes, heat the olive oil in a shallow pan and cook the leeks and garlic until just beginning to soften. Add the mushrooms and continue to cook briskly until the mushrooms are done and their juices running.

4 Add the potato flour or cornstarch off the heat, stir well, then gradually add the milk and stir until the sauce is quite smooth. Return to the heat and continue to stir until the sauce thickens.

5 Add the corn and hazelnuts and cook for 2–3 minutes to let the flavors amalgamate. Season.

6 Fill each crêpe with a spoonful of the filling (reserving some for later). Fold the crêpes over and arrange them in an ovenproof, nonmetallic dish.

7 Cover with plastic wrap and reheat in a microwave on full power for 2–3 minutes. Alternatively, cover with aluminum foil and reheat in the oven at 350°F for about 30 minutes. Reheat the remaining sauce and serve it with the crêpes. Sprinkle with parsley and serve.

--- COOK'S TIP ---

If filling the crêpes is difficult, place them in a dish and alternate with layers of the sauce.

--- NUTRITION NOTES ---

Per portion:

Calories	480
Fat, total	18.6g
saturated fat	3.3g
Protein	15.1g
Carbohydrate	66.2g
sugar, total	9.0g
Fiber—NSP	2.3g
Sodium	135mg

Green Lentils with Beans and Sun-dried Tomatoes

Although this dish can be eaten immediately, the flavor improves if left to "rest" for 24 hours. Reheat well before serving.

INGREDIENTS

Serves 4
¼ cup olive oil
4 medium leeks, finely sliced
2 large zucchini, finely diced
2 ounces sun-dried tomatoes, chopped in large pieces or, if you are on a solanacae-free diet, 2 ounces chopped black olives
¾ cup green lentils
scant 1 cup Retsina or dry white wine
1⅔ cups water
16 string beans, chopped roughly
soy sauce, which should be wheat-free tamari if you are on a wheat-free diet
chopped fresh flat-leaf parsley

1 Heat the oil in a pan and sweat the leeks and zucchini, covered, for 15–20 minutes or until the vegetables are well softened.

2 Add the sun-dried tomatoes, if using, the green lentils and the wine and water.

3 Bring back to a simmer, cover and cook for 20–30 minutes or until the lentils are cooked.

— COOK'S TIP —

This is a good dish to make in an electric frying pan if you find it easier. It can be cooked in and served from the same pan.

4 Add the string beans and the chopped black olives, if using, to the pan and continue to cook for another 5–10 minutes, until the beans are tender but not soft.

5 Season with soy sauce and sprinkle with parsley just before serving.

— NUTRITION NOTES —

Per portion:

Calories	338
Fat, total	18.8g
saturated fat	2.6g
Protein	12.3g
Carbohydrate	23.3g
sugar, total	4.4g
Fiber—NSP	6.1g
Sodium	133mg

Provençal Swiss Chard Omelet

This traditional flat omelet can also be made with fresh spinach, but Swiss chard leaves are typical in Provence. It is delicious served with small black Niçoise olives.

INGREDIENTS

Serves 6

1½ pounds Swiss chard leaves without stems
4 tablespoons olive oil
large onion, sliced or 2 tablespoons dried onion
2 eggs
salt and ground black pepper
sprig of fresh parsley, to garnish

1 Wash the Swiss chard well in several changes of water and pat dry. Stack four or five leaves at a time and slice across into thin ribbons (you can do this with scissors). Steam the Swiss chard until wilted, then drain in a sieve and press out any liquid with the back of a spoon.

2 Heat 2 tablespoons of the olive oil in a large frying pan. Add the onion and cook over medium-low heat for about 10 minutes, until soft, stirring occasionally. Add the Swiss chard and cook for another 2–4 minutes until the leaves are tender.

3 In a large bowl, beat the eggs and season with salt and pepper, then stir in the cooked vegetables.

4 Heat the remaining 2 tablespoons oil in a large nonstick frying pan over medium-high heat. Pour in the egg mixture and reduce the heat to medium-low. Cook the omelet, covered, for 5–7 minutes or until the egg mixture is set around the edges and almost set on top.

——— NUTRITION NOTES ———	
Per portion:	
Calories	135
Fat, total	10.3g
saturated fat	1.7g
Protein	5.9g
Carbohydrate	5.0g
sugar, total	3.9g
Fiber—NSP	2.9g
Sodium	185mg

5 To turn the omelet over, loosen around the edges with a rounded knife and gently slide it onto a large plate. Place the frying pan over the omelet and, holding them tightly, carefully invert the pan and plate together. Lift off the plate and continue to cook the omelet for another 2–3 minutes.

6 Slide the omelet onto a serving plate and serve hot or at room temperature, cut into wedges and garnished with a sprig of fresh parsley.

DESSERTS AND BAKED GOODS

This selection of delicious cakes and breads is suitable not just for an

arthritic diet but for wheat- and dairy-free diets as well. Try the

delicious Coconut Cream Dessert or Plum Crumble Pie for a rich

treat, or one of the three recipes based on fresh fruit for a more simple

dessert. The Zucchini and Double-ginger Cake is a must for arthritis

sufferers, as ginger can reduce inflammation in some people. The

breads are good, too; slice thickly and serve with honey or jam.

Oat Pancakes with Caramel Bananas

INGREDIENTS

Makes 10

⅔ cup unbleached all-purpose flour,
  sifted or, if you are on a wheat-free
  diet, rice flour
½ cup whole-wheat flour or,
  if you are on a wheat-free diet,
  chickpea flour
½ cup oats
1 teaspoon baking powder, wheat-free
  if you are on a wheat-free diet
pinch of salt
1 teaspoon brown sugar
1 egg
1 tablespoon sunflower oil, plus extra
  for frying
1 cup low-fat milk or, if you are
  on a dairy-free diet, soy, rice or
  coconut milk

For the caramel bananas
2 tablespoons butter, or sunflower oil if
  you are on a dairy-free diet
1 tablespoon maple syrup
3 ripe bananas, halved and quartered
  lengthwise
¼ cup pecans

1 Firstly, make the pancakes. Place the flours, oats, baking powder, salt and sugar in a large mixing bowl and stir them together.

2 Make a well in the center of the flour mixture and add the egg, sunflower oil and about a quarter of the milk.

3 Use a hand-held whisk to mix the ingredients well, then gradually add the rest of the milk to make a thick batter. Let rest for 20 minutes in the refrigerator.

NUTRITION NOTES	
Per portion:	
Calories	148
Fat, total	5.5g
saturated fat	1.9g
Protein	4.0g
Carbohydrate	22.0g
sugar, total	8.7g
Fiber—NSP	1.4g
Sodium	42.9mg

4 Heat a large, lightly oiled frying pan. Using about 2 tablespoons of batter for each pancake, cook two or three pancakes at a time. Cook for 3 minutes on each side or until golden. Keep warm while you cook the remaining seven or eight pancakes.

5 To make the caramel bananas, wipe out the frying pan and add the butter or oil. Heat gently, then add the maple syrup and stir well. Add the bananas and pecans to the pan.

6 Let cook, covered, for about 4 minutes, turning once, or until the bananas have just softened and the sauce has caramelized slightly. To serve, place two pancakes on each of five warm plates and top with the bananas and pecans. Serve immediately.

HEALTH BENEFITS
Bananas are an excellent source of energy, and they also contain potassium, which is essential for the healthy functioning of all the cells in our bodies.

Plum Crumble Pie

Polenta adds a wonderful golden hue and crunchiness to the crumble topping on this fruit-filled pie. Plums are a rich source of the antioxidant, vitamin E.

INGREDIENTS

Serves 6

1 cup unbleached all-purpose flour, sifted or, if you are on a wheat-free diet, rice flour
1 cup whole-wheat flour or, if you are on a wheat-free diet, chickpea flour
¾ cup brown sugar
1 cup polenta
1 teaspoon baking powder, wheat-free if you are on a wheat-free diet
pinch of salt
10 tablespoons butter or, if you are on a dairy-free diet, dairy-free spread, plus extra for greasing
1 egg
1 tablespoon olive oil
¼ cup oats
1 tablespoon sugar
custard or cream, to serve (optional)

For the filling
2 teaspoons sugar
1 tablespoon polenta
1 pound dark plums

1 Combine together the flours, sugar, polenta, baking powder and salt in a large bowl. Rub in the butter or spread with your fingers until the mixture resembles fine bread crumbs. Stir in the egg and olive oil and enough cold water to form a smooth dough.

2 Grease a 9-inch springform cake pan. Press two-thirds of the dough evenly on the bottom and up the sides of the pan. Wrap the remaining dough in plastic wrap and chill while you make the filling.

3 Preheat the oven to 350°F. Sprinkle the sugar and polenta into the pastry shell.

4 Using a sharp knife, cut the plums in half and remove the pits. Place the plums, cut-side down, on top of the polenta dough.

5 Remove the remaining dough from the refrigerator and crumble it between your fingers, then combine with the oats. Sprinkle evenly on the plums, then sprinkle with sugar.

6 Bake for 50 minutes or until golden. Let sit for 15 minutes. Remove the sides of the cake pan and slide onto a serving dish. Serve with custard or cream, if desired.

NUTRITION NOTES	
Per portion:	
Calories	535
Fat, total	24.3g
saturated fat	14.3g
Protein	7.0g
Carbohydrate	75.3g
sugar, total	33.4g
Fiber—NSP	3.0g
Sodium	208mg

---— COOK'S TIP —

The polenta dough can be made in a food processor if you find it easier.

Three Simple Fruit Desserts

Fresh Pineapple with Kirsch

INGREDIENTS

Serves 6
1 large pineapple
2 tablespoons sugar
3 teaspoons Kirsch or cherry brandy
mint sprigs, to decorate

1 Using a large sharp knife, cut off
the top and bottom of the
pineapple. Cut off the peel from top to
bottom and then remove the eyes,
cutting in a V-shaped wedge.

2 Cut the pineapple into slices and
remove the tough central core, if
desired. Arrange the pineapple slices on
a large serving plate. Sprinkle evenly
with sugar and cherry brandy. Chill
until ready to serve, then decorate with
mint sprigs.

COOK'S TIP

Pineapple can be tricky to peel, so use
canned pineapple if your hands are arthritic.

--- NUTRITION NOTES ---

Per portion:

Calories	46.5
Fat, total	0.0g
saturated fat	0.0g
Protein	0.2g
Carbohydrate	10.7g
sugar, total	10.7g
Fiber—NSP	0.5g
Sodium	1.0mg

Melon with Raspberries

INGREDIENTS

Serves 2
2 tiny or 1 small ripe melon
1 cup fresh raspberries
1–2 tablespoons raspberry
  liqueur (optional)

1 Cut off a thin slice from the
bottom of each melon to create a
stable base. If the melons are tiny, cut
off the top third and scoop out as much
of the flesh as possible from each top.
Cut the flesh into tiny dice.

2 If a larger melon is used, cut off a
thin slice from both the top and
bottom to create two stable bases; then
split the melon in half and dice the
flesh. In either case, scoop out and
discard the seeds.

3 Fill the center of the melon halves
with any diced melon and the
raspberries and, if desired, sprinkle with
a little liqueur. Chill before serving or
serve on a bed of crushed ice.

--- NUTRITION NOTES ---

Per portion:

Calories	46
Fat, total	0.3g
saturated fat	0.0g
Protein	1.4g
Carbohydrate	10.2g
sugar, total	10.2g
Fiber—NSP	2.0g
Sodium	43mg

Grilled Fruit Kebabs

INGREDIENTS

Makes 6
4 or 5 kinds of firm ripe fruit, such as
  grapes, pear and nectarine slices,
  mango and pineapple cubes and
  tangerine segments
2 tablespoons walnut oil
grated zest and juice of 1 orange, or
  omit if you are on a citrus-free diet
sugar, to taste
pinch of ground cinnamon or nutmeg
yogurt, sour cream, crème fraîche, soy
  milk or fruit coulis, to serve

1 Preheat the broiler and line a
baking sheet with aluminum foil.

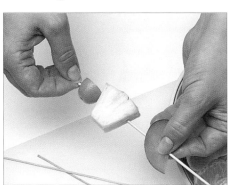

2 Thread the fruit onto six skewers
(dampened if wood), alternating
fruits to create an attractive pattern.
Place on the foil and brush with oil.
Spoon on the orange zest and juice, if
using, and sprinkle with the sugar and
spice. Broil for 2–3 minutes, until the
sugar just begins to caramelize. Serve
immediately, with your chosen topping.

--- NUTRITION NOTES ---

Per portion:

Calories	57
Fat, total	3.6g
saturated fat	0.3g
Protein	0.3g
Carbohydrate	6.0g
sugar, total	6.0g
Fiber—NSP	0.8g
Sodium	2.5mg

Coconut Cream Dessert

The soft, sticky texture of Thai fragrant rice makes it perfect for this dish. Desserts such as these are served in countries all over the Far East, often with mangoes, pineapple or guavas.

INGREDIENTS

Serves 4

scant ½ cup Thai fragrant rice, soaked
  overnight in ¾ cup water
1½ cups coconut milk
⅔ cup cream of coconut
¼ cup sugar
fresh raspberries and mint leaves,
  to decorate

For the coulis

¾ cup black currants,
  stems removed
2 tablespoons caster sugar
½ cup raspberries, thawed if frozen

1 Put the Thai fragrant rice and its soaking water into a food processor and process for a few minutes, until the mixture is soupy.

2 Heat the coconut milk and cream of coconut in a nonstick saucepan. When the mixture is on the verge of boiling, stir in the rice mixture. Cook very gently for 10 minutes, stirring constantly, then stir in the sugar and continue cooking for 10–15 more minutes or until the mixture is thick and creamy.

3 Pour the rice mixture into a shallow baking pan that has been lined with nonstick baking paper. Cool, then chill until firm.

4 To make the coulis, put the black currants in a bowl. Sprinkle with sugar and set aside for 30 minutes. Transfer to a sieve with the raspberries. Press the fruit through the sieve into a bowl. Add sugar to taste.

5 Cut the rice mixture into diamonds. Spoon the coulis onto each plate, arrange the diamonds on top and decorate with raspberries and mint.

NUTRITION NOTES	
Per portion:	
Calories	169
Fat, total	0.5g
saturated fat	0.2g
Protein	1.9g
Carbohydrate	42.9g
sugar, total	26.6g
Fiber—NSP	1.2g
Sodium	104mg

Zucchini and Double-ginger Cake

Both fresh and preserved ginger are used to flavor this unusual tea bread. It is delicious served warm, cut into thick slices and spread with butter or jam.

INGREDIENTS

Serves 10

3 eggs
generous 1 cup sugar
1 cup sunflower oil
1 teaspoon vanilla extract
1 tablespoon syrup from a jar of
  stem ginger
8 ounces zucchini, grated
1-inch piece fresh ginger root, grated
  or 1 teaspoon puréed ginger or
  1½ teaspoons ground ginger
3 cups unbleached all-purpose flour or,
  if you are on a wheat-free diet, ¾ cup
  rice flour and 2¼ cups pulverized oats
1 teaspoon baking powder, wheat-free,
  if you are on a wheat-free diet
1 teaspoon ground cinnamon
pinch of salt
2 pieces crystallized stem ginger,
  chopped
1 tablespoon brown sugar

1 Preheat the oven to 375°F. In a large bowl, beat together the eggs and sugar until light and fluffy. Slowly beat in the oil until the mixture forms a batter. Mix in the vanilla and ginger syrup, then stir in the zucchini and fresh, puréed or ground ginger.

2 Sift the flour (or rice flour and oats), baking powder, cinnamon and salt into the batter. Fold the dry ingredients into the zucchini mixture.

HEALTH BENEFITS

• Ginger has many beneficial attributes, not least of which is its ability to block the enzymes that lead to inflammation.
• Zucchini are a good source of betacarotene, vitamin C and folate.

3 Lightly grease a 2-pound loaf pan and pour in the zucchini mixture. Smooth and level the top, then sprinkle the chopped ginger and sugar on the surface.

4 Bake for 1 hour, until a skewer inserted into the center comes out clean. Allow the cake in the pan to cool for about 20 minutes, then turn out onto a wire rack.

NUTRITION NOTES

Per portion:

Calories	393
Fat, total	19.8g
saturated fat	3.11g
Protein	5.7g
Carbohydrate	51.2g
sugar, total	24.5g
Fiber—NSP	1.3g
Sodium	25mg

Apricot and Hazelnut Oat Cookies

These cookies have a chewy, crumbly texture. They are sprinkled with apricots and toasted hazelnuts, but any combination of dried fruit and nuts can be used.

INGREDIENTS

Makes 9

1 cup self-rising flour, sifted or, if you are on a wheat-free diet, 1 cup rice flour plus 2 teaspoons wheat-free baking powder
1 cup oats
scant ½ cup chopped dried unsulfured apricots
½ cup unsalted butter, or dairy-free spread if you are on a dairy-free diet, plus extra for greasing
scant ½ cup brown sugar
1 tablespoon honey

For the topping

2 tablespoons chopped dried unsulfured apricots
¼ cup toasted and chopped hazelnuts

1 Preheat the oven to 325°F. Lightly grease a large baking sheet. Place the flour (or rice flour and baking powder), oats and chopped apricots in a large mixing bowl.

2 Put the butter or dairy-free spread, sugar and honey in a saucepan and cook over low heat, until the butter melts and the sugar dissolves, stirring the mixture occasionally. Remove the pan from heat.

3 Pour the honey and sugar mixture into the bowl containing the flour, oats and apricots. Mix well with a wooden spoon to form a sticky dough. Divide the dough into nine pieces and place on the prepared baking sheet. Press into ½-inch thick rounds.

4 Sprinkle on the topping of apricots and hazelnuts and press into the dough. Bake the cookies for about 15 minutes, until they are golden and slightly crisp. Let cool on the baking sheet for 5 minutes, then transfer to a wire rack.

—— COOK'S TIP ——

Dried fruit such as apricots are easier to chop if you use scissors rather than a knife.

—— NUTRITION NOTES ——

Per portion:

Calories	276
Fat, total	11.9g
saturated fat	7.0g
Protein	4.4g
Carbohydrate	39.7g
sugar, total	11.7g
Fiber—NSP	2.4g
Sodium	104mg

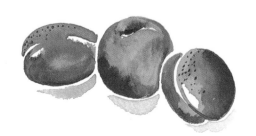

Wheat-free Brown Bread

This is a good bread if you are avoiding wheat and dairy products. It is similar in taste and texture to a fairly dense whole-wheat bread.

INGREDIENTS

Makes 1 loaf

3 cups brown rice flour
½ cup buckwheat flour
½ cup potato flour or cornstarch
1 teaspoon soy flour
½ teaspoon salt
2 teaspoons sugar
1½ teaspoons cream of tartar
¼ teaspoon baking soda
2 teaspoons active dry yeast
¾ ounce butter or, if you are on a
    dairy-free diet, dairy-free spread
1 egg
1 tablespoon sesame seeds (optional)

1 Preheat the oven to 350°F. Grease a loaf pan or a round cake pan. Place all of the flours, the salt, sugar, cream of tartar, baking soda and yeast in a large mixing bowl. Mix thoroughly.

2 Rub in the butter or spread, then stir in the egg and half the sesame seeds, if you are using them.

3 Combine ⅔ cup boiling water, with 1⅓ cups tap water. Stir this into the other ingredients.

4 Pour the mixture into the prepared pan. Sprinkle with the remaining sesame seeds, if using. Bake for about 40 minutes or until the bread is risen and a skewer comes out clean.

5 Cool in the pan for 5–10 minutes under a dish towel, then carefully turn out the bread onto a wire rack. Cover with a dish towel and let sit until quite cold before cutting.

COOK'S TIP

• The uncooked mixture will be very runny, but it will firm up during baking to produce a moist but compact loaf.
• If your hands are stiff you may find it easier to combine all of the ingredients in a food processor.

NUTRITION NOTES

Per loaf:

Calories	1,855
Fat, total	26.5g
saturated fat	12.7g
Protein	38.1g
Carbohydrate	36.0g
sugar, total	1.5g
Fiber—NSP	10.9g
Sodium	1,245mg

Rice Flour and Banana Bread

This is a great bread for those trying to avoid wheat and dairy products. It has more of the texture of a cake than of bread. It is delicious warm, served with jam or honey.

INGREDIENTS

Makes 1 loaf

2 bananas
5 ounces rice flour
2 ounces sunflower spread
2 teaspoons baking powder, wheat-free if you are on a wheat-free diet
1 egg
½ cup milk or, if you are on a dairy-free diet, soy milk

1 Place all of the ingredients for the bread in a food processor and purée until smooth. You can also use a hand-held blender in a bowl if you prefer. Meanwhile preheat the oven to 350°F and lightly grease a small loaf pan.

2 Spoon the mixture into the pan and bake for 35 minutes or until a skewer comes out clean.

3 Remove from the oven and let cool slightly. Turn out of the pan and place on a wire rack to cool, covered in a dish towel.

--- COOK'S TIP ---

You could easily turn this bread into a cake by adding 3 tablespoons brown sugar when you purée the bananas, and stirring in 2 tablespoons plump raisins or other dried fruit before it goes into the oven.

--- NUTRITION NOTES ---

Per loaf:

Calories	1,236
Fat, total	50.4g
saturated fat	15.3g
Protein	22.4g
Carbohydrate	172g
sugar, total	47g
Fiber—NSP	5.2g
Sodium	544mg

Information File

Useful Addresses

American College of Rheumatology
.600 Century place
Suite 250
Atlanta, GA 30345
Tel: (404) 633-3777
www. rheumatology.org

American Juvenile Arthritis
   Organization
1314 Spring Street, NW
Atlanta, GA 30309
Tel: (404) 872-7100
www.arthritis.org/ajao

The American Medical Association
515 North State Street
Chicago, IL 60610
Tel: (312) 464-5000
www.ama.org

The Arthritis Foundation
1330 West Peachtree Street
Atlanta, GA 30309
Tel: (800) 283-7800
www.arthritis.org

Arthritis National Research
   Foundation
200 Oceangate
Suite 440
Long Beach, CA 90802
Tel: (800) 588-CURE (2873)
www.curearthritis.org

The Arthritis Research Institute
   of America
300 South Duncan Avenue
Suite 240
Clearwater. FL 34615
Tel: (727) 461-4054
Fax: (727) 449-9227

Fibromyalgia Alliance of America
P.O. Box 21990
Columbus, OH 43221-0990

USA Fibromyalgia Association
Box 1483
Dublin, OH 43017
www.w2.com/fibrol.html

Lupus Foundation of America
1300 Piccard Drive
Suite 200
Rockville, MD 20850-4303
Tel: (800) 558-0121
www.lupus.org

National Institute on Aging
Building 31, Room 5C27
31 Center Drive, MSC 2292
Bethesda, MD 20892
Tel: (301) 496-1752
www.nih.gov/nia

National Institute of Arthritis and
   Musculoskeletal and Skin Diseases
National Institutes of Health
Bethesda, MD 20892-2350
Tel: (301) 496-8188
www.nih.gov/niams

National Osteoporosis Foundation
1232 22nd Street, NW
Washington, D.C. 20037-1292
Tel: (202) 223-2226
www.nof.org

The Road Back Foundation
P.O. Box 447
Orleans, MA 02653
Tel: (614) 227-1556
www.roadback.org

Sjogren's Syndrome Foundation
366 North Broadway
Jericho, NY 11753
Tel: (800) 475-6473
www.sjogrens.com

Glossary

ALA (alpha linolenic acid) – an essential fatty acid, found in oily fish, helpful in minimizing inflammation

antioxidants – nutrients or enzymes that neutralize free radicals in the body

cartilage – the protective cushion that separates bones where they meet in joints

free radicals – a chemical reaction that causes damage to the body's tissues

GLAs (gamma linolenic acid) – an essential fatty acid, found in some seeds, helpful in minimizing inflammation

NSAIDs (nonsteroidal anti-inflammatory drugs) – drugs that may be prescribed to help relieve inflammation and pain

prostaglandin – a chemical that can help control inflammation

solanacae – a family of foods (potato, peppers, eggplant and chilies) that may cause an allergic reaction in some people

synovial fluid – the fluid that lubricates a joint, allowing it to move freely

INDEX